Winning
the
Interview
Game

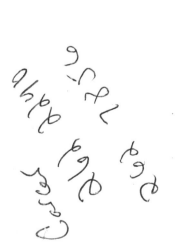

Winning the Interview Game

EVERYTHING You Need to Know to LAND the JOB

Alan H. Nierenberg

AMACOM

American Management Association

New York • Atlanta • Brussels • Chicago • Mexico City • San Francisco
Shanghai • Tokyo • Toronto • Washington, D.C.

Special discounts on bulk quantities of AMACOM books are available to corporations, professional associations, and other organizations. For details, contact Special Sales Department, AMACOM, a division of American Management Association, 1601 Broadway, New York, NY 10019.
Tel.: 212-903-8316.   Fax: 212-903-8083.
Web site: www.amacombooks.org

This publication is designed to provide accurate and authoritative information in regard to the subject matter covered. It is sold with the understanding that the publisher is not engaged in rendering legal, accounting, or other professional service. If legal advice or other expert assistance is required, the services of a competent professional person should be sought.

Library of Congress Cataloging-in-Publication Data

Nierenberg, Alan H.
Winning the interview game : everything you need to know to land the job / Alan
    H. Nierenberg.
          p. cm.
          Includes bibliographical references and index.
          ISBN 0-8144-7279-6
    1. Employment interviewing. 2. Job hunting. I. Title.

    HF5549.5.I6N54 2005
    650.14'4—dc22

                                                          2004029946

To Marsha, Tara, and Erin,
the most important people in my life

CONTENTS

PREFACE

If you are planning to interview for a job, then you have found the right book. You may be graduating from high school or college, transitioning between jobs, or seeking a new job while employed. Regardless of age, level of seniority, or area of expertise, this book will give you a strong competitive edge over the hundreds or thousands of competing candidates.

An Overview

Winning the Interview Game: Everything You Need to Know to Land the Job presents the interview for what it is—a game. There are many players who affect the outcome of this career game and you must learn how to deal with each group. Competing candidates and the judges representing everyone on the other side of the hiring desk are the major players. You must defeat your competitors and convince the judges that you are the one who can perform the job and should get the offer. The role of these players in the interview game and how you should interact with them are discussed in the book.

In describing how to prepare for and play the interview game, *Winning the Interview Game: Everything You Need to Know to Land the Job* will provide information not widely known by most job seekers. You will obtain first-hand knowledge from my experience on the other side of the interview desk as the current owner of an executive search firm, with previous experience as a vice president–human resources and a corporate hiring executive. I was also a job seeker several times in my career. I have personal experience with every approach presented in the book and have coached numerous job seekers whose interview experiences are reflected throughout its pages.

Although each interview is different, there are many components that are the same or similar. This book takes advantage of those similarities by providing a step-by-step approach to achieve your most important objective: to convince interviewers that you have the skills required to perform the job being discussed and that you are excited about applying those skills at the interviewer's company.

Empty Your Mind

Before learning a new system of self-defense, an aspiring martial artist must succeed in removing old habits from his or her mind. The student needs to absorb the philosophy and choreography of each class session, learn the basics, and not improvise in the early years of instruction. Adaptation to the student's physical abilities will occur over time. And so it is for this text. Prepare for the interview, develop and execute your strategy, apply proven tactics and you will be able to adjust your approach for each interview after you master the basics.

And don't be afraid to explore every opportunity to play the interview game. Put out of your mind previous negative experiences and prejudices as well as self-imposed obstacles that may prevent you from finding a new job. Do not say that you will *never* work at another startup, another Fortune 500 company, or another company that requires driving more than an hour to the office or one that requires mass transportation to get there. Go with the flow and you will be pleasantly surprised with the outcome.

Many self-imposed restrictions in a job search usually are based on previous experiences that went bad. Move through the search process as quickly as you can and analyze each situation in which such obstacles are slowing you down. In virtually every interview opportunity, you should be able to identify job acceptance criteria that will be strong incentives to accept a particular position, regardless of the perceived negatives. For example, if you were a casualty of a dotcom that ran out of funding, you should now be prepared to reduce the risks in a new company by insisting on a sign-on bonus and a higher salary before accepting an offer. Do not refuse to interview for a job that might be a three-hour drive from home. If you succeed in getting an offer, you have the option to demand temporary living expenses for a period of time, home visits each weekend, a telecommuting option, and a subsequent relocation with your family. If the company refuses to satisfy your request, you have the ultimate power to reject the offer and continue your search.

Very often job seekers will not go on interviews if the title is one level below their previous title or compensation is 10 percent or 20 percent below what they recently earned. This is the wrong move. Do not let either of these issues stop you from going on a first interview, which is so difficult to obtain. You might exceed your expectations by impressing interviewers and causing a hiring manager to realize that an upgrade in title and/or salary is warranted. Consider every opportunity to schedule an interview before eliminating any job possibility.

The Game

The more you play the interview game, the better you will get, and the more job offers you will receive. As in any game, you must learn the rules, understand the players, and know how to reach the finish line. The book is organized into three parts.

Part I: Let the Game Begin: The Preparation

This part of *Winning the Interview Game: Everything You Need to Know to Land the Job* prepares you for your first interview. Chapter 1 describes the rules of the game and follows a hypothetical job seeker named Susan who has just scheduled an interview. The chapter identifies information to gather and knowledge to acquire before the interview.

Part II: Game Plan: Interview Strategies and Tactics

Part II takes you almost minute-by-minute on Susan's interview. This part provides insight into the typical interview and its common variations. Chapter 2 describes the initial ten minutes of the interview where the first and most critical moves of the game are executed. These early moves are important because they create a great first impression, establish rapport, and set the tone for the remainder of the interview. Chapter 3 describes how to respond to the barrage of questions throughout the middle of the interview and provides guidance on how to deal with sensitive and difficult issues interviewers like to address. Chapter 4 takes place in the last ten minutes of the interview and includes how to leave a lasting impression. The chapter discusses how to handle the different types of interviewers, such as peers and subordinates. In addition, advice is provided for winning in other interview settings, such as a telephone or videoconference interview. Chapter 5 provides guidelines on how to maneuver through second and subsequent interviews and how to differentiate yourself from the competition.

Part III: Winning Move: Enjoy the Moment

Part III describes the final hurdles for job seekers to overcome before an offer is presented. Chapter 6 addresses salary and reference issues and walks you through the landmines of negotiating, juggling, accepting, and rejecting an offer. A description of background checks and an approach to convince the company psychologist you have the right personality for the job are also presented. The chapter and the game end when you show up on the first day of work and make the wonderful transition from being unemployed to being a success in your new job. The last valuable piece of information presented in the book is how to plan for the next interview game while you are in the process of settling into your new job.

ACKNOWLEDGMENTS

Thank you to my many close and personal friends and family too numerous to mention whose support was caring and continuous.

The following individuals deserve a special thank you.

Nick Battista, a great friend, inspired me to write this book. He was my mentor and provided encouragement and advice throughout the project. The book would not be in print without him. I am truly indebted to his support and wish him the best in bringing his four novels to print.

Bob Diforio is an agent only superlatives can describe. I am very fortunate to be the recipient of his persistence and personal reassurances that led to placing this project with AMACOM, the highly regarded publishing arm of the American Management Association.

Ellen Kadin, Senior Acquisitions Editor at AMACOM Books, had the wisdom to recommend revising the scope of my first proposal to what appears in this book. The professionalism and support of the AMACOM marketing, sales, publicity and administrative staff are also very much appreciated.

Members of the Executive Forum, a select group of senior executives devoted to sharing expertise as they move through their careers. It has been and continues to be a privilege to be a job search resource for Executive Forum members, and I will always appreciate the support and encouragement that I received from the membership throughout this book project.

Dr. Genie Laborde for taking the time to provide insightful advice on Neuro Linguistic Programming concepts, which she so clearly presents in her book *Influencing With Integrity*.

Ken Meyer, a prominent executive recruiter and former human resources executive, who reviewed an early draft discussing these important gatekeepers and provided valuable suggestions.

Julie Jansen, a friend, speaker, coach, trainer, and consultant, who provided a book on proposal writing and offered helpful and ongoing advice resulting from her own success publishing *I Don't Know What I Want, But I Know It's Not This, A Step-By-Step Guide to Finding Gratifying Work*.

Joanne Pobiner, Certified Image Consultant, President of Paramount Image Management, and professional member of the Association of Image Consultants International, who contributed her outstanding advice on how to step forward with a winning appearance and achieve a notable first impression.

Chuck Duvall, a specialist in videoconference systems, who provided excellent advice for interviewing at a videoconference center.

PART I

LET THE GAME BEGIN: THE PREPARATION

Chapter

1 | Prepare for Perfection: Before the Interview

Susan finally got her first job interview after an intense four months of searching. Four months of searching to get a one-hour job interview is a realistic statistic in these times. It could be another few months, or more, before she has the next interview. This places immense pressure on her and other job seekers to learn and apply effective interview skills.

Susan must convince the first interviewer, and possibly additional five or ten interviewers, that she is the candidate who should receive the coveted job offer. Read on to uncover the secrets of getting beyond the front-line human resource professionals and executive recruiters (the gatekeepers) to the hiring manager and a job offer.

How Susan Got the Interview

One morning Susan received a call from a friend she contacted a month earlier, "Hi Susan, it's Tom. An acquaintance of mine is the vice president of human resources at a local company, and they are looking for a marketing manager. If you are interested, I will give you the contact information." She obtained the contact name, Scott Gilbert, vice president-human resources and graciously asked Tom if she could assist him in any way. Susan was excited when she hung up the phone. She immediately reviewed the company's web site and called Scott to introduce herself as Tom's friend. Scott's administrative assistant, Amanda, answered the phone and requested that Susan e-mail a copy of her résumé. Within an hour, Susan received a call from Scott's internal recruiting manager. The purpose of that call was for the recruiting manager to ensure that Susan had the experience necessary to warrant an interview with Scott. The telephone interview and other interview formats are discussed in Chapter 4. Susan made a compelling case for an interview with Scott, and she had one week to prepare before the scheduled interview. This was the call Susan worked so hard to receive. The following chapters walk you through the steps she took to win the interview and a job offer.

Rules of the Game

Interviewing is like a board game—competing players all have the same starting point and the winner is the player who accumulates the most points along the way. The starting point for the interview game is when a job seeker has a scheduled interview with a company executive or search professional who is trying to fill a specific job. The game ends on the first day of a new job.

The rules are simple. An interviewer hosts the meeting in an office setting where a friendly conversation takes place between two people. The interviewer takes the lead role and asks candidates a series of questions mainly about qualifications to perform the job. Other topics include delving into personality and determining how likeable the job seeker will be to the staff. The interviewer evaluates each response and determines if the candidate will be invited back for another interview. From the candidates' perspective, they must respond to each question with completely honest answers. Any lies appearing in a résumé or told to an interviewer will automatically disqualify the candidate at any time. If misinformation is uncovered after a new job begins, the new employee will most likely be fired.

Job seekers must focus on the end game of getting a job offer. Contrary to a commonly held belief, the best qualified candidate does not always win this game. Although an offer can be attributed to many factors, such as who a candidate might know, the winning candidate usually exhibits the following qualities:

➤ Possesses basic skills and experience required for the position.

➤ Satisfies the needs of the recruiter, human resources professional, hiring manager, and other interviewers.

➤ Establishes rapport with interviewers and creates the perception of being like them.

➤ Exhibits impressive displays of energy and passion.

➤ Demonstrates a personality compatible with the hiring manager and the responsibilities of the position.

➤ Possesses qualities that differentiate the individual from competing candidates.

➤ Presents a detailed understanding of company products, culture, industry, and politics better than most employees.

If you have these qualities, you are among possibly three to ten competitors who are at the starting gate and waiting to be interviewed by company management. Arm yourself with inner confidence and knowledge of the interview journey that lies ahead.

Game Preparation

Winning players begin the game with an intense interview preparation. How the newly acquired knowledge gained as part of the interview preparation is used during the interview separates the great players from the rest of the group.

Capable management consultants have a particular skill that is extremely relevant to interviewing. Sarah just joined the consulting staff of a prestigious management consulting firm. She has an M.B.A. from a top school and four years of information technology experience at a manufacturing company. She completed her company's consulting orientation program and was given her first assignment. She had three days to prepare for an initial meeting with the vice president-information technology at her first client. The company manufactured battery products, and Sarah knew nothing about the battery business. What was she to do? Sarah had been told that her company's clients expect consultants to know all about their business, and she had to convey that impression at a meeting in just three days. She spent most of her waking hours learning everything about the company, industry, product lines, management, and customers. Consultants do this all the time. In her first client meeting, Sarah was able to create the perception that she had a good understanding of the industry, its strengths, weaknesses, opportunities, and threats. Why did Sarah go through this grueling preparation?

➤ To satisfy client expectations of understanding their business.

➤ To instill self-confidence.

➤ To perform her consulting assignment in a stellar manner.

Job seekers should have the same motivation to convince interviewers that they understand and value the company's business. Hiring managers prefer candidates with a passion for and an understanding of their business over candidates who have no idea what the company does. Spend hours and days of research gathering information identified in this chapter with the objective of learning more than your competition. Use this knowledge to differentiate yourself and to create a perception of extensive knowledge. Your goal in this preparation is to know as much or more than most employees in the company you are about to interview with.

All job seekers should have a good understanding of the industry in which they work and the functions performed in the position for which they are interviewing. Sufficient knowledge and background information must be demonstrated to convince interviewers that you understand the business and will have a very short learning curve to become productive. Conveying information during an interview is like answering a question on a final exam—it makes no difference if you learned the answer the night before or the month before, as long as you have the correct answer. To ensure that a comprehensive approach is taken to conduct the required research, organize this project around the company and its industry, the profile of the people you might meet, and the pertinent aspects of the position for which you are interviewing.

The Company and Its Industry

This information is helpful regardless of the job being sought. It makes no difference if you are interviewing for the most junior or the most senior position or for any functional area of expertise, such as administration, financial, marketing, human resources, or sales. You will acquire an aura that differentiates you from common candidates.

➤ *Corporate Background.* Mission, strategies, history, office locations, annual report (call company shareholder services department for a copy).

➤ *Overview of Company Organization.* Number of employees. In which industries do company divisions compete? In what division is the position for which you are interviewing?

➤ *Press Releases and Industry Analyst Opinions.* Excellent information source to impress interviewers. Check several times, particularly on the day of or day before the interview.

➤ *Major Products and Their Competitive Advantages.* Have you used any products, do you have a hobby that involves the company's products, have you visited company stores or branch offices? Learn why the company's products are better than competing products. Call the company marketing department for public information provided to customers.

➤ *Revenue.* Worldwide revenue by country. Where does the money come from? You might have extensive experience with a particular source.

➤ *Company Strengths, Weaknesses, Opportunities, and Threats.* This SWOT analysis is performed in most M.B.A. programs.

➤ *Competitors and Competing Products.* You might be very familiar with a competitive product and can convert that knowledge to a positive impression during an interview.

➤ *Research and Development Programs.* Are these projects at the leading edge of their industry? Are adequate resources devoted to research and development?

➤ *Current and Target Customers.* You might have personal contacts that could provide you with this difficult-to-obtain information.

➤ *Overview of the Industry and Where the Company Appears Relative to Size and Growth.* Is this a growing or stagnant industry? Is the company a leader or industry follower?

➤ *Financial Data and SEC Filings.* Extensive information is available for public companies, including backgrounds of board members and the executive team often with compensation, recent earnings, income statement, balance sheet, ROI, and financial facts.

➤ *Company Accounting, Law, or Consulting Firm.* You might know someone to call for networking purposes.

➤ *Partnerships, Mergers, Acquisitions, Joint Ventures, and Other Activities that Could Eliminate Current Job Openings or Create New Ones.* Is the company in an acquisition mode or is it looking to be acquired? You might have contacts at other companies where these activities are being planned.

➤ *Social Responsibility.* Identify organizations supported by the company; you might be involved with the same organizations and identify networking contacts.

➤ *Career Opportunities.* Awareness of other job openings and position descriptions might provide insight into what personal and professional qualities are being sought.

People Profiles

The first people you should find out about are the interviewers. This background information is less important for recruiters because most have a common purpose to find, evaluate, and submit qualified candidates to client management. You will only meet a recruiter once. However, it will be helpful if you can talk to someone who was interviewed previously by the same recruiter or recruiting firm.

Gathering intelligence on company executives is a critical component of advance preparation. Determine the background of the interviewers, the management team, and the board of directors. Become as familiar with these backgrounds as employees might be. For company managers, look for commonality with your background, like having previously worked for the same company, holding similar titles, attending the same schools, belonging to the same professional or not-for-profit organizations, or performing a particular function (e.g., writing visual basic programs, negotiating alliances with other companies or selling the same products). Prepare for each interview by summarizing and presenting your experience in a way that mirrors the profile of each interviewer. More about this in Chapter 2.

Details About the Position

Some fortunate job seekers will be given a detailed position description that can serve as a roadmap for interview preparation. Alternatively, others might get an oral summary or a one-line description. Determine the requirements as best you can, including the functional responsibilities, technical experience and political interaction with other departments, parent organization or other companies. Try to obtain some of this information in the telephone call that resulted in scheduling the interview. Always ask for a written position description if there is one.

The position description might identify elements of which you have limited knowledge, and the preparation period should be used to learn more about these areas so that you can carry on a basic conversation. If you are seeking a programmer or information technology position and have limited knowledge of a required language or software package, then learn it before the interview. Find a tutorial on the web and learn the software package's functionality and features to enable you to discuss during your interview. Some financial positions require experience with the Sarbanes-Oxley Public Company Accounting Reform and Investor Protection Act. Even if you have no hands-on experience with the requirements of the SOX, as it is often referred, learn the basics of how public companies must be compliant and you can still impress an interviewer.

Where to Begin

There are two obvious starting points. The first is the recruiter or person who introduced you to the company. Most recruiters have met or spoken with human resources executives and hiring managers to obtain the position specifications. The recruiter should share background information on key staff (i.e., tenure with the company, previous experience, personality) and annual reports and other company literature that they have.

The person who led you to the job opportunity may have personal relationships with one or more company employees. When you call to thank this person for the introduction, mention your upcoming interview. In that conversation, ask for the same information you would expect from a recruiter, and you may benefit from some excellent insights into company interviewers and products.

The next place to go is the company's web site. Follow every path and link. Some companies will make your job simple by having a robust web site with just about everything there is to know about the company. Go through the purchase process for a product and stop just short of entering your credit card number. See first hand how easy, or difficult, it is for customers to buy something. Print selected information that you want to read and reread until the moment of the interview.

There are numerous web sites that offer information on companies, industries and just about anything required for a research project. Go to the advanced search feature of popular search engines (e.g., www.ask.com and www.google.com) and enter key words such as company name, industry, product name, or other words or phrases that would identify some aspect of the target company. Search engines will produce web sites that supposedly have the answers.

Be creative. The Internet has a wealth of information, and it is clearly the place to conduct much of your research. However, job seekers should not limit their research to computer-driven searches. Time should also be spent in a public library, where the research librarian could identify material to review. There are numerous directories in print and electronic form that list names and contact information for human resources executives, hospital industry decision makers, industry associations, and many more types of listings.

Graduating college seniors should use the career placement office and college graduates should use the alumni career centers at their undergraduate and graduate schools. An outplacement firm is an excellent source for a senior executive whose previous company included that service as part of a severance package. Career counselors at outplacement firms offer advice on where to find information to prepare for an interview.

Networking Groups

In addition to seeking out colleagues, friends, current and former business associates, members of professional organizations, alumni associations, and any other contacts that might know about the company or individuals with whom you will be interviewing, networking groups can be a very effective source of information. Members could refer you to associates employed at the company's banks, accounting firm, investment bankers, customers, suppliers, or they might know classmates, neighbors, or friends of key management staff. The challenge of finding insider contacts is not as daunting as you might think.

Marty was a member of a financial networking group comprised of financial analysts, controllers, and chief financial officers. He attended regular biweekly meetings and had gotten to know many of the forty members who are actively looking for new jobs. These are people he can trust. As part of his preparation for an upcoming interview, Marty decided to ask if anyone in the group had a contact at the company where he had an upcoming interview. At the meeting, he asked the members to respect his confidence and not to discuss the situation outside the room. Three members referred excellent sources. Marty spoke with each referral and he played his inside information very effectively during the interview. This is a common occurrence with networking groups, and job seekers can derive tremendous benefits through membership in selected groups.

It would be a major coup if you were to be referred to a person who worked, or works, at the company. Imagine if you were to find a former incumbent who is now at another company! Someone at a competing organization could be equally valuable. Another prize would be someone who interviewed at this company for the same or similar position. Be diligent and persistent in obtaining information about the company with which you will be interviewing.

What to Do with a Networking Connection

All of this contact information is powerful. It can uncover interviewer personalities, company culture, and an almost limitless number of facts for use during an interview. There is an issue to consider if the contact is an employee of the company or a close personal friend of an employee. Consider a worst-case scenario even if you request the person to keep your meeting confidential. How might your candidacy be affected if the interviewer scheduled to meet you uncovers the fact that you met with an employee to extract company information? You should assess the extent to which you can trust your source.

On the positive side, an inside contact could be the proverbial pot of gold at the end of the rainbow. You could learn the real scoop that helps you get a second interview. If you find out that one of your interviewers has a terrific sense of humor, then you might want to inject a bit of humor during that interview. If the interviewer is said to be a conservative, serious person, then you will want to be very business-like. If you decide against reaching out to the employee contact before the first interview, you can reassess the situation before the second or subsequent interview, if you get past the first one.

Behavior-Based Interviewing

Recruiters, both contingency and retained, and human resources professionals responsible for recruiting may interview hundreds, or more than a thousand, job seekers each year. That intense experience puts most of these professionals at the top of their trade when it comes to conducting interviews and assessing job seeker skills. Assessments are based on a combination of the first impression and an interviewing style known as behavior-based interviewing. The vignette strategy described in the next section of this chapter provides an effective approach for job seekers to handle a behavior-based interview.

Behavior-based interviewing has been around for many years. The generally accepted premise is that past behavior and performance are reasonable predictors of future behavior and performance. Behavior questions avoid yes or no answers and require that you respond with an actual experience or accomplishment. There are no hypothetical "what if" questions. There are only open-ended questions that require a description of actual experiences. Follow-up questions can be asked if additional details are required. The following are sample behavior-based questions related to a range of functional skills:

➤ Describe a recent accomplishment where you saved your previous company money. A follow-up question might be: What was your specific role, and how were you recognized by company management?

➤ How did you win your largest sale?

➤ What marketing steps did you take to achieve a 24 percent market share?

➤ How did you avoid an employee revolution when a company merger resulted in a change of employee benefits?

➤ Describe a quality improvement you implemented and the results achieved.

➤ Describe how you prepared a complex financial model and communicated the analysis to management.

➤ Describe a win-win situation you negotiated and indicate what each side believed it won.

➤ Describe the steps you took as a systems analyst when you developed the company web site.

➤ Describe what you did as the vice president-human resources when an employee informed you of a sexual harassment situation.

➤ How did you motivate others during the project you just described?

➤ Describe your most difficult experience handling a customer and tell me the outcome.

➤ Describe a situation where a co-worker had a difficult personality and how you handled it.

> Describe a situation when you took an opposing position and achieved your objective.

> What were the significant steps you took to reduce expenses and achieve a profitable year?

> What was an important decision you made, how did you arrive at it, and how did you implement it?

> How did you get your vice presidents to accept a recent strategic initiative?

The Vignette Strategy

Vignettes, or brief descriptions, should be used in every interview to describe knowledge, accomplishments, and experiences. A vignette should convince interviewers that you know what you are talking about and should replace the simple yes or no response to interview questions. Résumés are the first place vignettes should appear, interview preparation is where a career of vignettes should be summarized, and interviews are where vignettes should be presented.

The format of these mini-stories should include a company problem, action taken by you, and the outcome that benefited a previous employer. The vignettes, like the example that follows, should take between one and three minutes to recount. Interviewers may ask you to elaborate on certain aspects of the vignette or move on to another question.

> *The company was poised to establish a new business venture and customers were confused about the direction the company was taking. **(problem)** I organized a team comprised of internal experts and line managers from the new venture. I then led the team in defining and communicating the new venture's mission and strategy to existing and potential customers. **(action taken)** The new venture exceeded revenue projections in the first three months of business because of an informed customer base and an effective strategy. **(resulting benefit)***

Vignettes should be organized in a logical order, perhaps by position requirement, to validate your qualifications for the job to be filled. For each required strength and skill, prepare a few factual vignettes based on your experiences and achievements. Sequence the vignettes from the most recent to the oldest without using dates. Document the vignettes to be delivered as arrows in a quiver during the interview.

These mini-narratives should convince interviewers that you have done what the job requires and have the ability to perform these same tasks again. They also serve to create a perception that you will have a short learning curve. It is essential to exhibit a sense of accomplishment, pride, and satisfaction when presenting each vignette to an interviewer.

Recent graduates will not have years of experience to create many vignettes. Often, just a few very relevant vignettes can impress interviewers. There are surprisingly many sources from which recent graduates can prepare vignettes, including individual accomplishments and skills obtained in part-time jobs, volunteer work, or internships. Responsibility as the captain of a varsity team can certainly produce leadership stories. Participating in an extracurricular activity, traveling for a semester abroad, or volunteering for a mentoring program are great sources for vignettes. Courses taken and projects completed, such as a complex financial spreadsheet, an engineering design, or a visual basic program are excellent examples. The key to being a top candidate is in the delivery—be focused, energetic, and exhibit passion.

Vignette Preparation and Examples

In addition to preparing vignettes relating to your functional skills and accomplishments, consider other qualities you can offer a prospective employer. Interview preparation should include vignettes that demonstrate your leadership, teamwork, supervision of a difficult employee, and a difficult project completed.

Vignettes should be typed and taken with you to the interview. Prepare the list on white bond 8½- by 11-inch paper and insert the paper into a notepad as the second page, hidden from the interviewer's view. The vignettes will be used extensively in response to interviewer questions discussed in Chapter 3. The following are abbreviated samples of vignettes organized by functional discipline. They are brief, focused, and should take less than two minutes to present.

Operations

➤ Decision-support tools were absent in a Fortune 500 company. I utilized operations research techniques to build and implement decision-support systems. I developed an inventory control model and produced annual savings of $20 million.

➤ Quality review procedures were nonexistent in a complex business plan for a new venture. I initiated and completed the quality review of processes and procedures based on ISO 9000 quality principles and oversaw implementation of its recommendations. The board of directors subsequently approved the plan.

➤ The cost of travel services provided by an independent travel agent was prohibitive. I evaluated the legal implication of terminating the agreement and assessed the feasibility of creating an internal travel function. I successfully negotiated a release from the contract, developed an internal travel function, and saved $1 million annually.

Business Development

➤ The growth of a fledging business required alliance partners to reduce costs and increase revenue. I initiated discussions with fifteen potential partners, evaluated their business proposals, and entered into partnership agreements with four organizations. The company experienced significant growth.

Financial

➤ Expense and capital budgets were not controlled and there was a risk of exceeding authorized limits. I instituted expense reporting and control procedures for a $30 million budget and documented the objectives and benefits of each project. This action increased management confidence and introduced effective controls over spending.

➤ The company had cash flow problems and was soon to have problems meeting payroll. I evaluated and negotiated banking relationships, gave numerous presentations, and obtained a $15 million line of credit.

Marketing

➤ A significant rollout for a major product was planned, but emphasis was placed on technical aspects and less on marketing requirements. I determined customer needs, developed and implemented marketing recommendations, and introduced the product at a well-publicized media event. The rollout was successful and customer acceptance was excellent.

➤ The decreasing number of subscribers was causing a decline in revenues, and something was needed to keep the publication solvent. I executed marketing programs, which integrated print, TV, direct mail, and cross-promotion opportunities. This initiative increased revenues by 15%.

Information Technology

➤ The growth in the number of worldwide offices led to a confusing array of incompatible software and hardware configurations. I obtained the confidence of worldwide management and developed a global information technology plan with standard applications and systems. I then obtained funding and implemented the plan during a two-year period, which improved efficiencies and generated additional revenues.

➤ The information technology (IT) department's systems and databases were unreliable, the systems staff was not experienced, and costs were out of control. I led a reorganization of the IT department, reducing the number of locations from seven to five and the number of IT employees from 350 to 225. I developed new procedures to optimize performance, reduce the workforce, and control project quality. Resulting savings was in excess of $8 million annually.

➤ The contract negotiation process was too lengthy and disadvantageous to the negotiating team. I led a systems project to design and develop a contract management system used by chief negotiators and lawyers when negotiating large contracts with business customers. Implementation of the system resulted in reducing the negotiating time by 75 percent and I was given the annual company productivity award.

Elevator Drill

An important element of preparation is a two-minute and a thirty-second version of your background and skills supporting the position being sought. The drill is recited upon being introduced to interviewers and other players anywhere, anytime, even during a brief elevator ride. The new acquaintance you met on the fifth floor could be your next boss. This introduction should be well rehearsed and continuously focused and refined. A version of the same drill is used during an interview in response to the "tell me about yourself" request discussed in Chapter 2. The following are the elements that should be included in the elevator drill:

➤ *Names of a Few Companies Where You Recently Worked, Particularly if the Companies Are Recognized and Well Known.* Working previously for a prestigious company creates the perception that the job seeker passed a tough professional test and obtained credible experience.

➤ *Industries in Which You Have Experience (e.g., Consumer Goods, Technology, Healthcare).* Stating one or two industries in which you have in-depth knowledge would be a big plus, especially if the person you are speaking with works in one.

➤ *Functional Position—Type of Position Being Sought (e.g., Web Developer, Controller, Engineer, Trainer, or Chief Executive Officer).* Support the desired functional position by stating two or three strengths that are widely understood and marketable (e.g., for human resources: expertise in benefits, compensation structure, and 401-K administration).

➤ *Unique Qualification—Factors that Differentiate You from Competitors.* This is an opportunity to differentiate you from competitors by citing experiences or credentials that provide a competitive edge over other job seekers. Some examples include a combination of Fortune 500 and entrepreneurial experience when applying to a small firm, foreign language skills when approaching an international firm, or a recognized certification, such as the Certified Public Accountant (CPA) or Certified Management Consultant (CMC) designations.

Do I Ask Questions?

Yes! However, you should be in sell mode and convince interviewers that you have value to add and your previous experiences can satisfy what the company needs. Your goal in the first interview is to ask questions that show your interest and understanding of the position requirements. Establish rapport and impress interviewers before walking on the question tightrope.

As part of preparation, identify three or four questions that focus on clarifying the requirements of the position so that you can respond with your relevant experience. A by-product of preparing for the interview and asking questions is that the information you gather can be used as the basis for subsequent due diligence. Examples of questions you might ask during the interview could be: What would you view as a major accomplishment in the first six months? or Which departments does the position interact with?

A key principle is to resist the urge to ask questions that have even a remote appearance of being due diligence related, for example, how many vacation days, what are your financial projections, and what is the personality of the person my position reports to. Asking questions aimed at due diligence in early interviews will likely kill your candidacy. These questions could embarrass interviewers because the answers may reveal an inability to raise capital, an unprofitable business, employee morale problems, or other sensitive disclosures. All such questions are too presumptuous and probing and should be asked after an offer is received, at which time you have every right to be informed of such critical information. Besides, these questions distract interviewers from assessing your experiences and skills.

Anticipate Questions to Be Asked

Every interview is filled with questions for the job seeker. Although Chapter 3 includes commonly asked questions and the rationale for recommended responses, do not stop there. Anticipate questions you might be asked about your industry, its trends, recent developments and current news items. Drilling down into the foundation of your functional and technical skills is an approach taken by some interviewers. Go to the company's web site and review open jobs they are trying to fill. Identify common job requirements and be sure to prepare for any questions that might be related to those skill requirements found in more than one job description. Review publications that list hundreds of possible interview questions. Identify a manageable number of most likely questions, list them with your planned response and practice reciting your answers in a natural, unrehearsed manner.

Practice, Practice, Practice

The best way to become proficient with interview techniques is to practice being a job seeker in an actual or simulated interview situation. Most job seekers have limited interviewing experience and should not use a real job interview as a practice session. This a great opportunity to seek help from a friend who is a recruiter, human resources executive, or hiring manager with considerable interviewing experience. Create a situation where you are interviewing for a job and your friend is conducting the interview. At the conclusion of the session, both of you will identify areas that require additional practice. Some examples might be to increase direct eye contact, speak with a confident voice, avoid slouching, be more animated, and appear more interested.

An even better approach is to rehearse using a video camera. Viewing the playback, everyone is surprised at how they sound and appear on screen, and additional areas for improvement usually are apparent with this technique. An improvement on this approach is to ask four or five friends to watch the videotaping and playback. You will get the most honest feedback from good friends.

You are now ready for your first interview. In Chapter 2, we rejoin Susan as she begins the interview game in her one-on-one interview with a vice president of human resources.

PART II

GAME PLAN: INTERVIEW STRATEGIES AND TACTICS

Chapter 2 | Find an Opening Connection:
Establish Rapport

Although no two interviews are alike, each experience is identical in one respect. All interviews have a beginning, middle, and end. Chapters 2, 3, and 4 walk you through the important first interview, almost minute-by-minute, with a job seeker named Susan, as if there were a personal coach sitting beside her. Susan succeeded in scheduling a face-to-face interview with the vice president-human resources (VP-HR), Scott Gilbert, who has been searching for a few months for a director of marketing.

The approach taken by Susan throughout this first interview would be almost identical for a first interview with an executive recruiter, a hiring manager, senior management, peer, subordinate, and other company employees. There are some differences in approach for these interviews, which are discussed in Chapter 4.

View from Behind the Desk of the
Vice President—Human Resources

Human resources (HR) departments serve as both the company entrance and exit for the employee base. Because corporate recruiting is one of the many responsibilities of the HR department, HR management is usually aware of and coordinates staffing needs in all company departments. This is an excellent group to target for networking purposes.

The top HR executive has two very distinct reporting responsibilities. The first responsibility is to company senior management. In this role the HR executive is responsible for overseeing all aspects of company human capital including ensuring productivity, promoting employee satisfaction, serving as a job counselor to all employees, protecting the company from employee-related lawsuits, and being a conduct between senior management and employees by communicating vision and values.

25

The second reporting responsibility is to serve as the employee ombudsman. Employees should know that one or more HR staff members are available to discuss personal or personnel issues that could affect their performance. This often occurs when employees are not comfortable discussing sensitive issues with immediate supervisors.

Recruiting at large companies may result in the hiring of thousands of new employees annually, while small companies may hire only three or four employees each year. In both extremes, the hiring process is critical to the future growth and health of the company. A wrong decision that results in the termination of a new employee and restarting the recruitment process could cost tens of thousands of dollars. Such costs place great pressure on the HR staff to hire the right people and establish procedures to keep them productively employed.

With respect to recruiting, HR professionals are evaluated by line managers on closeness of candidate qualifications, timeliness of identifying potential candidates, and retention of new hires. Line managers expect HR professionals to find qualified candidates fast—the planned start date is always yesterday. This pressure might affect how closely job requirements are adhered to, and job seekers should try to uncover how eager an HR executive might be to send résumés to hiring managers. Under certain circumstances HR might send résumés to hiring managers that satisfy, say, 80 percent of the specifications, rather than forward only "perfect" candidates. This pressure can work favorably for job seekers.

In Susan's situation, the VP-HR must be convinced that she satisfies most, if not all, of the position requirements. His reputation is on the line with peers on the management team, his boss (the president), and the hiring manager's team. He must also assure himself that Susan's personal demeanor fits the corporate culture and will be acceptable to most employee personalities. Scott is interviewing other candidates, and he will only send to his line managers the résumés of candidates who most closely satisfy the position requirements, exhibit a strong interest in performing the job, and demonstrate an acceptable personality. He must be confident that each recommended candidate impresses his line managers and will not be an embarrassment. The hiring manager and the person to whom Susan will report is the vice president-marketing. This is the person who has the final decision to hire or not to hire. On the morning of the interview, the only information Scott has about Susan is her résumé, the favorable results of a brief telephone screen by the HR manager, and the knowledge that she was referred by a trusted acquaintance.

The Morning of the Interview

A good night's sleep should be a priority before this important morning because there is much for Susan to do before her 10:00 A.M. interview. The morning hours should be focused on preparing to make an excellent first impression. There is only one chance for this to happen. Visualize positive interaction between you and company interviewers and you will convey good feelings and improve the odds of a positive outcome.

If you speak with anyone on the morning of the interview, make sure that the person is supportive, positive and upbeat. Pretend you are about to attend a martial arts lesson on how to defend yourself against someone with a baseball bat. Get that adrenalin flowing. Be alert. Feel good about yourself. Be relaxed and maintain your inner confidence. You can do it.

Get Dressed for Success

Conservative clothing is in and beach thongs are out. First impressions are formed mostly by nonverbal communications including appearance, facial expressions, eye contact, posture, and, least of all, spoken words. Before you utter a single word, your appearance already has. First impressions are formed within thirty seconds, many times subliminally. According to Joanne Pobiner, Certified Image Consultant and professional member of the Association of Image Consultants International (AICI), "significant value judgments are made based solely upon appearance, for example, economic status, education, level of success, sophistication, integrity, credibility, likeability, and even moral character." The visual integrity of job seekers is clearly at stake.

Do not be misled by the many companies that permit casual attire for their employees. Casual business dress often turns out to be casualty dress in interview situations. Remember that you are not yet an employee, and you must go through a hazing period before you are permitted to dress like one. Styles vary by profession as well as region of the country. If you are interviewing for a job in the advertising or entertainment industries, you may be able to dress less formally than in the financial services industry or legal profession. No matter what your area of expertise may be, a suit is the best choice for men and women job seekers.

You might want to go into an upscale clothing store and find a knowledgeable salesperson to recommend an appropriate business outfit for an interview. You do not have to buy it there, but you should get a good idea of what's in and what's not. Another source of advice could be a certified image professional found on the AICI website *www.AICI.org.*

Check the company web site or annual report for the company that is interviewing you. View pictures of the management team and see if there is a company dress code. Although employees in some industries may wear rather lavish attire, conservative style is almost always acceptable. The most important aspect about your appearance for an interview is that you think you look great. If you look and feel great, your heightened self-confidence will likely make a favorable impression upon your interviewers.

Joanne provides the following guidelines for a winning appearance.

General

> Grooming is paramount. One's hair must be clean and neatly trimmed. If a woman's hair is longer than shoulder length, pull it back or wear it up.

> Do not overlook your fingernails, since they speak volumes about your personal care and attention to detail.

> The best advice for smokers interviewing for an office position is to stop smoking when looking for a job. It is almost impossible to hide the smell of smoke on clothing or when breathing.

Men

➤ Wear a relatively new dark suit that fits well, is clean, pressed, and made of a quality fabric. Wearing a navy blue or charcoal gray suit are your best choices for an interview. The same colors are also viewed favorably internationally.

➤ A lightly starched white, cream, or powder blue shirt just picked up at the cleaner worn with a conservative tie is preferred in most office situations.

➤ It is important for the collar of the shirt to fit comfortably. If purchasing a new dress shirt, close the top button and you should be able to slide two fingers between the neck and the collar. This allows for shrinkage.

➤ Your tie should enhance your own personal coloring as well as your suit. A conservative pattern and a quality fabric such as silk will be very acceptable. Be sure that your tie is knotted well and hugs your throat. Its length should reach to your belt buckle.

➤ Although your shoes are at ground level, their impact is great. Lace-up wing tips are a smart choice with your suit. You will want to make sure that the heels and soles are in excellent condition and that the shoes are well polished.

➤ Select socks to match your trousers, not your shoes. Be sure that they are high enough to cover your calf so that no skin comes peeking out if you should happen to cross your legs.

➤ Facial hair might be fine for a few professions, but if you have the slightest doubt, shave it off. Mustaches are more acceptable than beards and less acceptable than being clean-shaven. If you think that your mustache is appropriate, make sure that it is neatly trimmed without snow or ice from your commute. Review the company web site or annual report and count the number of men on the management team with beards and mustaches to help you make this decision.

➤ Avoid jewelry except your wedding band and a moderately priced watch, if you normally wear one. Do not even think of wearing an earring or any facial jewelry for most office positions.

➤ Use cologne and/or aftershave lotion very sparingly or not at all. If the scent is distasteful to your interviewer, you could lose many game points.

Women

➤ Wear conservative, quality, well fitting clothing. A relatively new dark skirt or pant suit is a wise choice.

➤ Long-sleeved blouses in white, cream, or pastel blue work well. Avoid sleeveless and low-cut tops. Although you will wear a jacket over the blouse, be aware of the message that you may send.

➤ Basic leather pumps are a favorable choice for shoes. Avoid sandals and very high heels. Wobbling into an interview does not project confidence and stability. Your shoes should be the same shade or darker in color as your skirt or pants.

➤ Natural-colored hose are always a safe bet. Hose colors should be the same shade as your shoes or lighter.

➤ Give special attention to your make-up so that it is applied neatly, blended well, and not overdone.

➤ Jewelry should be kept to a minimum. Engagement and wedding rings, moderately-priced watches, and earrings no larger than a quarter are fine. Avoid all facial jewelry.

➤ Avoid perfume or use it very sparingly. Why chance an embarrassing sneezing fit?

Last-Minute Preparation

Before you leave home for the interview make sure you have everything you need. Interviewer and receptionist names, address, telephone number, and directions to the company are critical. Take a new 8½- by 11-inch notepad and carry two ballpoint pens. Bring three copies of your résumé, but offer it only if asked. The notepad and selected reference material about the company should be placed in an attaché case in good condition, which can be the larger type with a handle or a small one that can hold the notepad and other papers. Make sure there is room for additional material company representatives might provide. The page or two of vignettes you prepared should be placed under the top sheet of the pad so that only you are able to read these notes. Buy the morning paper and read the headlines and the business section for interesting, noncontroversial stories that might be brought up in the course of conversation.

Get There Early

Plan to arrive at the company facility ten to fifteen minutes before the scheduled interview, otherwise you will be stressed and lose the advantage for a positive first impression. The best approach is to arrive forty-five minutes to an hour early. Go to the company location so that you will know exactly where it is, and walk or drive to the nearest coffee shop or eating establishment. Buy a muffin and coffee, or something comparably light, and just relax for half an hour. Review your notes from the company research, rehearse your elevator drill and vignettes, and think positive thoughts about the upcoming interview. Before you leave the coffee shop, go to the rest room and take a last minute look at yourself, particularly your smile. That will be your most widely used weapon during the interview, so make sure there are no food remains. Arrive at the reception desk about ten minutes before the scheduled time.

The Reception Area

As Susan enters the building and takes the elevator to the reception area, she correctly imagines that there are four hidden video cameras focused on her as she enters the building and approaches the reception desk. A staff member she is about to meet might be walking into the building right next to her or standing in the same elevator.

The first words in the interview game are about to be spoken. Susan goes directly to the company receptionist and says, "Good morning. My name is Susan Arnold and I have a ten o'clock appointment with Scott Gilbert." She is animated, friendly, relaxed, and shows her smile. She wants to make an excellent first impression with everyone she meets. The same receptionist could be welcoming Susan on the next visit, and, more importantly, Scott may request the receptionist's opinion of her after the interview. This happens more than most job seekers realize. The receptionist will offer coffee or a cold drink and direct Susan to a waiting area. It is best to decline any beverage to minimize risking an embarrassing spill. Susan immediately writes the receptionist's name on the notepad page behind the vignettes for future reference. It would be a major relationship builder if she could use the receptionist's first name when calling Scott again. Susan reviews company literature while waiting for Scott.

This brief wait is a tremendous opportunity to observe employees as they parade through the reception area. Are they neatly attired, professional in appearance, friendly to each other, do they appear to have a sense of purpose in their strides, or are they just meandering through the office waiting for five o'clock? Susan seizes the opportunity to strike up a conversation when approached by an employee who asks if she is being helped. She stands to thank the person for the offer, says her name, and indicates that she has an appointment with Scott Gilbert. When the employee responds with his name, Susan promptly asks which department he works in and then ends the conversation without appearing too inquisitive. Susan immediately writes down the person's name and department beneath the receptionist's name on her notepad. What a wonderful gesture that was.

Job seekers should be alert to establishing relationships during the brief period in the reception area. These relationships can be very helpful during second or subsequent interviews that might take place over the next weeks or months. In another situation, Mike was interviewing for a management position and waiting in the reception area for an interview with the CEO. Mike was a U.S. citizen and British by birth, and he had that distinctive accent many Americans enjoy listening to. Mike decided to initiate a conversation with the receptionist. He had a good reason. The receptionist also had a British accent and Mike was curious to find out where the receptionist was from. They both grew up in the suburbs of London and established a great rapport. Coincidently, the receptionist was also the administrative assistant to the CEO. Everyone knows how difficult it is to have a telephone conversation with a company executive, especially a CEO. Mike never seemed to have any trouble during the remainder of his interview process. Yes, he received an offer and accepted it.

The Moment of Truth

A few minutes before 10:00 A.M., Susan recites her mantra, which is the focused objective she must achieve during this important first interview. Accomplishing this objective should result in a second interview for Susan.

Interview Objective

To convince each interviewer that you have performed all the position requirements and you have a passion for doing them again at this company.

mANTRA

The receptionist takes Susan to a conference room where Scott is waiting. Susan begins the short walk and takes two deep breaths in through her nose and out slowly through her mouth. Stress, nervousness, and anxiety are expelled and relaxation and confidence dominate her feelings. This technique may be repeated unobtrusively, as needed, during the interview. Scott makes his first move. He stands to greet Susan and extends his hand. Susan leans a bit toward Scott; responds with a firm handshake, not bone crunching or wimpy; gives Scott direct eye contact and a wide smile; and with confidence says, "It's a pleasure to meet you." She has just applied the critical ingredients of a lasting first impression and perfectly countered Scott's opening move. Susan must now sustain that impression by establishing rapport. She knows how to play the game.

Susan takes a seat, places the notepad discreetly on her lap, and leans a bit forward in her chair toward Scott conveying a keen interest in his opening remarks. She places both feet firmly on the floor, sits upright with shoulders slightly back, arches lower back with eyes making direct contact and hands relaxing on the chair's arm rests. In an infrequent change of position, she may rest the bottom edge of her hands on the table with open palms facing towards each other angled downward. All of this while appearing relaxed and comfortable. She avoids making a fist, placing palms flat on the table or slouching in her chair. Good posture is essential to convey the desired qualities of being alert and energetic.

If the interviewer is seated on a higher chair and looks downward to make eye contact, accept the situation and let the interviewer assume the authoritative position. Do not stretch, change chairs, or in any way attempt to reach the same height as the interviewer. If you are uncomfortable, try to put up with it for the remainder of the interview. If your position is unbearable, then look for a graceful way to get comfortable only after you have successfully established rapport.

Scott gives Susan his business card and initiates small talk with the purpose of creating a friendly atmosphere and a free-flowing, interactive dialogue. From his perspective, he wants Susan to be relaxed and to speak without any "screening" of her remarks. Susan does get more relaxed but she is still in complete control over what she says and how she says it. Her mantra flashes through her mind. She is upbeat, energetic, confident, and enthusiastic in discussing the weather, ease of getting to the office, a news headline, and other mundane topics. Susan included on her résumé a conversational knowledge of French, and Scott asks her where she learned to speak the language. She replies that she lived in Paris for three years as a teenager when her father was transferred there on a special assignment. Scott travels to Paris often and the next few minutes of discussion about France clearly established the rapport and a memorable bond between the two.

Susan is careful not to make any negative comments during the entire interview and does not reply to questions with a simple yes or no. The image for Scott to remember from the moment he meets her should be a very positive, confident, professional person. Susan is a firm believer of applying Pareto's Law of 80 percent and 20 percent to the interview process. She tries to get the interviewer to speak 80 percent of the time and she will speak only 20 percent of the time. The 20 percent will be focused on achieving her interview objective. She is able to shift discussion to Scott by providing brief, direct responses lasting one to three minutes each. Interviewers may also take time to discuss a particular topic as a prelude to another question. The more a job seeker speaks, the more likely it is that a faux pas will occur.

Consistent use of positive statements and avoidance of mentioning negative experiences are critical factors in establishing rapport early in the interview. I was a guest speaker at a roundtable of human resources executives on a morning where the rain was causing tremendous floods and traffic was delayed everywhere. The session started twenty minutes late to enable most attendees to arrive. As typically occurs in presentations with small groups, the chairperson asks everyone to present a one-minute introduction. One senior executive began his introduction with a description of driving to the meeting in a heavy rain and searching thirty minutes for a parking spot. On the train ride back to my office, I summarized the background of the attendees. There was one person whose name, area of expertise, and company were a complete blank, except for the horrendous drive he had that morning.

All the Right Moves

Scott changes his tone from casual to business-like after about ten minutes and begins to describe the company and the marketing position for which Susan is interviewing. Susan is impressed with how smoothly he moved to begin the "formal" part of the interview, and she follows his lead. He repeats the same objective for the position as Scott's recruiting manager did one week ago when scheduling the interview. Scott described the company's magazine publishing business and the marketing director's responsibility to expand the subscription base. Susan knows it is her turn to speak when Scott asks one of the most frequently asked opening requests in an interview. Tell me about yourself. He might have asked, "Let me hear your elevator drill" or "Give me an overview of your background."

Susan is prepared to give the same answer for almost any opening question. She summarizes her experience and accomplishments that she knows to be relevant to the position requirements. If she were not previously informed of the position requirements, then Susan would take her best guess at one or two possible requirements and state her accomplishments relevant to those requirements. The response should be no more than one or two minutes.

> I have twelve years of marketing experience in the publishing and entertainment industries. In the previous six years I worked for two publishing companies, about

three years each. In the first company I was a marketing manager and in the second company I was promoted to marketing director. In both situations, I was responsible for increasing the subscriber base of the flagship magazine and succeeded in achieving significant increases for each of my publications. The positions were fantastic and I was constantly challenged to identify new techniques and approaches to increase subscriber growth. My recent company was sold and the new owners are not relocating anyone to their headquarters across the country.

This was presented with confidence and passion. Susan focused on her mantra and described how she had performed what she believed to be the position requirements and stated how much she enjoyed the challenges. The most recent six years are when Susan performed the requirements she believes are important for this position. Although she is proud of her earlier accomplishments, she did not mention seemingly unrelated, and possibly dated, accomplishments unless asked to do so. Describing such a great recent job would prompt Scott to ask why she left that situation, so she pre-empted the question by mentioning the company relocation in her reply. Interviewers almost always ask why job seekers left their last job, and this technique of stating the reason in brief, matter-of-fact terms early in the interview, without being asked, often avoids a lengthy discussion about this sensitive subject. Her response was a winning move.

Scott and the recruiting manager informed Susan that a key requirement is to increase the subscriber base. She would be remiss to think that that was the only skill the company expected of a new marketing director. Susan must be sure she identifies all of the position requirements early in the interview if she is to achieve her objective. There is only one sure way to find out if there are other requirements. The moment she completes her reply to Scott's opening question, without allowing Scott time to pose another question, Susan continues with the following question. If Scott had a different opening question, then Susan would have responded with a brief, direct answer and moved to a form of the following question: "Scott, you mentioned that increasing the subscriber base is a key requirement.

Would you please share any additional requirements so that I can better focus my answers for the remainder of our discussion?"

Susan asked the question in a modest, nonconfrontational, confident tone. Scott replied that direct marketing experience was also required. Susan thanked Scott for that information and immediately informed him that direct marketing was an integral part of her recent job and included both the use of the Internet and traditional direct marketing. She casually writes "direct marketing experience" on her notepad and feels good about the succession of winning moves she has made.

Although each interviewer will likely agree with most of the stated requirements, many will have a different perspective on what the new employee should do. These unique requirements for each interviewer are critical for job seekers to uncover, and the follow-on question asked by Susan should be asked in a similar form to every interviewer.

Susan is playing the game well. In the first ten minutes she has succeeded in accomplishing the following:

➤ Made a good first impression with the receptionist and the interviewer.

➤ Established rapport.

➤ Replied to the first interview question with relevant accomplishments.

➤ Avoided discussing irrelevant and out-dated experiences.

➤ Uncovered a new position requirement possibly unknown by other candidates.

➤ Recorded requirements inconspicuously on a notepad.

This sets up the strategy to play relevant vignettes for the remainder of the interview as Susan moves to Chapter 3 and the interrogation that follows.

Establishing Rapport

Rapport is one of those feelings that can be described as "you will know it when you see it." It results in establishing trust, a bond, a link, or a connection with someone. Many recruiters, human resource professionals, and hiring managers place great emphasis on hiring candidates with whom they have established a good rapport; therefore, job seekers should do anything possible to improve their odds of achieving this connection with interviewers. Establishing rapport should take place early in the interview and requires understanding and practicing the principles involved before applying them during the interview. Its importance is so critical that a job seeker with all substance and no rapport will not get an offer.

The following are some qualities that interviewers need to feel comfortable with before rapport can be complete:

➤ Will supervisors, peers, and subordinates like you?

➤ Do you have a friendly personality?

➤ Will you treat others with respect even when they disagree?

➤ Can employees trust you and confide in you with sensitive business or personal issues?

➤ Do you have excellent people skills?

➤ Can you reach consensus without confrontation?

➤ Can you describe your accomplishments without being condescending?

Demonstrating that you are a person others would enjoy working with every day is an attribute of winning job seekers. Although some may succeed in being well liked without much preparation or coaching, no one should underestimate the need to establish and maintain rapport with each interviewer at each meeting.

Rapport is a prerequisite for achieving a desired interview outcome, and it is the result of a positive communications experience between job seeker and interviewer. Establishing a connection, applying neurolinguistic programming (NLP) techniques, and executing a first impression are powerful tools for establishing rapport. Good things happen to prepared people.

Make a Connection

Establishing rapport in the first five to ten minutes sets a positive tone for the remainder of the interview. Job seekers should identify a connection with each interviewer as part of interview preparation or do so on-the-spot during the interview. Possible connections include attending the same school, working at the same company, sharing a common acquaintance, vacationing at the same resort, living in the same town, enjoying the same favorite restaurant, or something else that would provide the interviewer with a positive reminder about your visit.

If the meeting were to take place in the interviewer's office, you can scan the room for pictures or desktop items to provide a hint of the interviewer's interests. Be certain it is the interviewer's room before commenting on any observations. Care should be taken when observing pictures of the interviewer with other people. Someone's late husband could be in a desktop picture and a cloud would cover the room if you asked who the person was. If you have been to the location of a family picture, you could mention that it was one of your favorite trips—trying to initiate discussion about your visit to the same place.

Neurolinguistic Programming (NLP) Background

Neurolinguistic programming (NLP) principles can establish a connection between job seeker and interviewer that leads to rapport. These principles were defined in the 1970s by John Grinder, then a linguistics professor at the University of California, Santa Cruz, and Richard Bandler, a psychology student at the university. The term *neuro* refers to how we use the neurological senses of sight, hearing, feel, taste, and smell to represent everyday experiences. *Linguistic* refers to spoken words used to communicate our experiences and thoughts to others. Organizing our words and ideas into models/patterns defines *programming*.

Grinder and Bandler developed NLP models based on the behavior exhibited and the language used by outstanding leaders who achieved incredible success communicating with and influencing others. Different models work best for each circumstance and the models are continuously improved.

An important application of NLP is the ability to create harmony and conformity required for good rapport between two individuals. NLP techniques applied to achieve rapport are especially useful for job seekers during an interview.

The following discussion of NLP is the result of distilling principles and techniques from resources listed in the bibliography and identifying practical applications for job seekers. The information presented is the tip of the NLP iceberg and is intended to arouse job seeker interest because of its powerful ability to improve job seeker communications with interviewers and networking contacts. Take the time to review the cited resources, attend NLP seminars, consider coaching services of an NLP practitioner, select the techniques that fall within your comfort zone, and practice them with friends and family before your next interview. After sufficient practice, appropriate application of these techniques should improve your ability to develop rapport and to achieve your desired interview outcome. Insufficient practice can result in using NLP inappropriately or incorrectly, which could kill all chances for rapport.

NLP Concepts

The following are a few NLP concepts that can be helpful to job seekers for establishing rapport in interview situations. Changing an interviewer's negative behavior, albeit more difficult, is also presented.

> *Likeness.* People are generally more willing to accept and understand you when you look as they look, speak as they speak, do as they do, think as they think, or achieve a likeness in some way. Be like the interviewer. For example, an interviewer with a strong southern accent from Georgia working for a company in Wisconsin will immediately have a favorable bias toward a candidate with the same accent and rate of speech. How many times have you noticed someone with the same tie or dress and made a humorous remark to the person? That coincidence could have been a rapport-setting experience.

Congruency. Congruency, or alignment, between a point being made and body language that accompanies it is critical. If you really believe in what you are saying, then congruency of facial expression or body movement comes naturally. This is demonstrated, for example, when someone describes a happy experience accompanied by a wide smile; however, the same description presented by someone with a scowl throws the story's truthfulness into question. An example where congruency applies to job seekers is during the presentation of the elevator drill. A smile accompanied by passion and an upbeat personality would demonstrate congruency for someone satisfied with their drill. That same message carried consistently throughout the interview demonstrates congruency.

Similar Outcomes. The odds of NLP techniques being successful increase when both the job seeker and interviewer have similar desired outcomes. This occurs with interviewers more often than job seekers realize. When hiring professionals commit company time and resources to meet face-to-face with a handful of job seekers, most interviewers usually have a strong desire to find a winner so that the time-consuming interview process can come to an end. That desire forms the basis for a shared outcome with job seekers who must then convince interviewers that they have the needed experience.

Mirroring. NLP studies have shown that when a person mirrors (exhibits) similar speech patterns, breathing rates, or body positions with a second person, the first person becomes aligned, or in synch, with the second person. The result is that the second person often perceives that he or she has something in common with the first person and begins to form a bond. This alignment generally results in establishing a rapport between the two people because they approach the same state of likeness. Job seekers can apply this concept by using the following mirroring techniques:

* *Voice Matching.* According to Dr. Genie Z. Laborde in *Influencing with Integrity, Management Skills for Communication and Negotiation,* "Matching the other person's

voice tone or tempo is the best way to establish rapport in the business world. Tones are high or low, loud or soft. Tempos are fast or slow, with pauses or without pauses."* This can be accomplished in an unobtrusive manner with negligible risk of being observed. If an interviewer or networking contact is speaking at a rapid rate, then you should increase your rate of speech so that it approaches the other person's rate. Speaking at the exact rate might be noticeable and unnatural, and it is not necessary. The same technique should be performed for someone who speaks at a slower rate than you normally do.

In a similar manner, you should approach the loudness or softness of the interviewer's voice without being concerned of a precise match. The risk to a job seeker who normally speaks softly is twofold. The interviewer might assume the candidate has little confidence, and it would be annoying to the interviewer to continually ask the job seeker to repeat what was said.

- *Breathing Rate.* Observe the other person's breathing rate and synchronize your breathing to the same rate. If you are successful at voice matching, then you might automatically fall into the same breathing rhythm without realizing it.

- *Body Positioning.* Do not to attempt to maneuver into the same facial, hand, feet, or body position as an interviewer. A deliberate move to match body position is too risky and will be awkward, unnatural, and noticed. However, if in the midst of a conversation you observe that a match has occurred in a natural manner, then you have accidentally established rapport.

Care should be taken to avoid matching exactly or mirroring the extremes (e.g., very loud voice or fast rate of speech) because that would be too obvious and offensive. Rather, approach the interviewer's actions in a subtle way to achieve a similarity with the mirrored factors.

---

* Genie Z. Laborde, *Influencing with Integrity, Management Skills for Communication and Negotiation* (Palo Alto, Calif.: Syntony Publishing, 2001), p. 30.

Sensory Language Communications. When two people speak with each other, the goal is to have one or both exclaim "I understand exactly what you mean. We speak the same language." That referenced language is based on the use of our neurological senses. Individual experiences and activities are recorded and represented in terms of our senses of sight, hearing, touch, smell, and taste. The predominant senses are the first three, which are referred to as visual, auditory, and kinesthetic. The remaining two senses are not as widely used in business decisions therefore are not included in discussions on sensory language. The following are examples of how we use our senses to express our thoughts:

- *Visual.* "That report was a bright idea." "The project looks like it will succeed." "Where do you see your progress in a few years?"

- *Auditory.* "That report sounds terrific." "Bells went off when you mentioned his name." "That description is just what I needed to hear." "The project status has too much static." "Is all the noise about you being unhappy true?"

- *Kinesthetic.* "I have a good feeling about that report." "That was really a moving experience." "You made a smooth transition to your current job." "Are you as rough around the edges as everyone says?"

As we describe experiences, individuals tend to favor one of these representation systems over another and the result is reflected in our words (i.e., the linguistic component) that describe the experiences. A key factor in using one system over another is that people will most likely relate to and understand their favored system spoken by another person. That is the path to establishing rapport. Determine early in the interview which sensory language is favored by the interviewer and use the same sensory representation in your responses and remarks.

Communicating in the same sensory language is the equivalent of speaking Spanish in Spain or Italian in Italy. The result should be an understanding of each other and a perception of "likeness" between job seeker and interviewer. Likeness leads to rapport. Using the same sensory language as the person to whom you are speaking needs be done only several times in a one-hour interview to be effective. When interviewing several people at once, the safe approach is to use the three major sensory languages: visual, auditory, and kinesthetic interchangeably to achieve maximum rapport with the group.

Change Negative Behavior

There are some interviews that just do not go well and you are convinced that you will not be invited for a return visit. In some instances, an interviewer's body language can project a negative attitude about the interview. Be on the lookout for signs of unwelcome behavior and take action to salvage the interview by changing that behavior. Job seekers should be wary when interviewer's exhibit a "prove it to me" or "I don't believe you" attitude. A common body position that could convey this attitude is when arms are firmly folded across the chest for a noticeable period of time and the interviewer is not smiling. No matter what you say, it appears that the interviewer has no interest or does not believe you. Another situation that could derail an interview is a bored, impatient, or uninterested interviewer. Body language that could reflect these feelings includes frequent yawning, doodling, or watching the clock. At the same time these negative telltale signs are being observed, job seekers must be careful not to exhibit any of these fatal moves.

In this extreme situation, or where you simply have a feeling that you are not well liked by the interviewer, there is an approach you might try to change interviewer behavior. Attempt to change the communication pattern by causing temporary confusion or disruption of the interviewer's thought process. Actions that might create a communication interruption include bending down to pick up an intentionally dropped item, interrupting the interviewer and then apologizing, excusing yourself to walk across the room to remove an item from your coat, or creating some diversion from the current discussion. Events outside your control may be helpful, such as the phone ringing or someone entering the room. Stand up to greet the newcomer.

A positive scenario resulting from this pattern break could result if the interviewer asked, "Where were we?" You should be prepared for this and respond with a totally different topic of your choice that relates to a positive experience or vignette that would impress the interviewer with your closeness of fit to the position requirements.

The following are reasons why two candidates were rejected from consideration after interviewing for the same senior management position:

- "She was poised and confident with excellent leadership skills, but she appeared too reserved and not outgoing enough."

- "He was outgoing, extremely intelligent, a quick thinker, and understood our business, but he had an edge to his personality that might rub people the wrong way."

Both interviewed with eight members of the senior management staff and their rejection had nothing to do with qualifications. They were both highly rated in that area but each failed to establish a likeness with their interviewers. If both candidates mastered NLP techniques, they might have been able to modify their behavior during the interview and experience a different outcome.

First Impression

There is no second chance for a first impression—it lasts a long time. Susan demonstrated the key ingredients the moment she met Scott. The magic of a first impression must be sustained throughout the interview, so repeat some of its elements such as smiling frequently; maintaining direct eye contact without staring; and vary the amount of feeling, warmth, passion, and excitement in every response. Communicate clearly, present a professional, mature image, be modest, and display pride and an inner confidence when describing accomplishments.

Be on alert at all times for a first impression opportunity. You might meet your next interviewer or supervisor anywhere on company premises from the reception area to the restroom.

Be positive about everything, including previous companies worked, bosses, travel time to the interview, everything. There should be no complaints or negative words mentioned, not even a negative thought. Use compliments to demonstrate that you are a friendly and thoughtful person and be careful not to overdo your friendliness. Refer to an item of clothing, the desk, a picture, or something you observe in the office and be sincere when acknowledging its beauty or other quality. Describe your use of a company product and mention its good features, especially when comparing it to a competitive product. Flattery can be an integral part of the first impression.

Susan is ready for the onslaught of questions characterized by the middle portion of the interview.

Chapter 3

Meander Through the Middle:
Bulging with Questions

This chapter spans the middle thirty or forty minutes of a one-hour interview. The typical format during this part of the game is that the interviewer asks questions and the job seeker answers them; the interviewer determines if the job seeker can perform the position requirements and would enjoy doing so, and the job seeker creates the perception that he can and will; the interviewer decides if she likes the job seeker personally and professionally, and the job seeker wears a friendly face with matching personality. Be a chameleon and play the interview game.

If you have basic qualifications and some interest in the position, you can be a viable player. Remain in the game if you think you can perform the job requirements, even if you are not completely sure you want to work for the company or the interviewer. A lot can and does happen during the elapsed time of the interview process. The company may initiate changes to the position requirements or you might do so when negotiating an offer, either of which could increase your interest level. The best possible outcome is that you receive an offer, are satisfied with its terms, and accept. The second best outcome is that you receive an offer, negotiate objectionable conditions in your favor, and accept the offer. The worst possible outcome is that you do not receive an offer or the company will not satisfy your objectionable conditions.

Susan is about to continue her interview with Scott. But first, there are some issues with which Susan and other job seekers should become familiar before moving through the question and answer period of the interview game.

Power of Perception

There is only one winner selected from among the many competing candidates, and you want to be that person. Perception is the weapon of choice. Based on real experiences, describe how you previously performed the position requirements and state that you can and want to do them again. The vignette is the vehicle for relating your experiences.

When questions are asked, provide a brief, direct answer followed by one or more vignettes to demonstrate how you previously performed a similar position requirement mentioned in the question. Use vignettes that support position requirements for as many questions as possible. Present a common theme to your answers, a consistent story, and a very narrow focus for each response to demonstrate that you have performed each of the position requirements. "Brainwash" the interviewer with vignettes and you might create the perception that you can do much more than is required. Everyone likes a good story, and they enable interviewers to sell your candidacy to other members of the management team.

Following are two effective techniques to create a positive perception:

➢ *Read relevant articles as part of interview preparation and refer to them in your response to an appropriate question.* Kathy got her first interview with a software company a month after receiving a computer science degree. The company developed and sold computer-aided design (CAD) software and one of the requirements was installation and user training experience with the company's CAD offering. Kathy had not worked with that company's package so she conducted extensive research during interview preparation for information on the CAD software. She found a press release describing a successful client installation and reviewed the company's web site and other literature describing the features of the software. When the interviewer asked Kathy if she previously installed the CAD package, her response was honest. She replied that although she did not install the software, she was very knowledgeable about its features, benefits, pricing, training requirements, and other factors. She proceeded to describe the installation experience appearing on the company's press release and she spoke about the software's key features and benefits to the end-user. The interviewer was impressed and she was invited for a second interview.

➤ *Cite opinions others have of you by referring to yourself as the third party.* This technique has more credibility than you would get by describing your own strengths. My recent boss often told other team members to ask for my help when managing projects. That sounds better than speaking about yourself, which could come across as boasting or exaggerating.

Use of Preparation Knowledge

The purpose of gathering information described in Chapter 1 is to impress each interviewer, and, when an offer is obtained, to help job seekers reach the decision to accept the offer or not. Use it wisely. Knowledge about the company, its products, management, and culture must be played back in such a way that interviewers are convinced that the job seeker knows as much as a well-informed employee. Although job seekers might have obtained company knowledge in the few days and evenings prior to the interview, the best use of the information is to convey it as if it were known for longer that just the previous day or week. This is accomplished by stating company information as a matter of fact, as an employee might do. An excellent technique is to mention a competing product by telling the interviewer how much better a company's product is viewed in the marketplace. That will demonstrate your knowledge of competitors and could be a home run. Besides, a little praise goes a long way.

Facing an Experienced Interviewer

It is safe to assume that most gatekeepers are experienced interviewers because of the large numbers of candidates interviewed each year. Although there are exceptions, the same assumption should not be made for hiring managers. Many experienced interviewers use the behavioral interviewing technique to evaluate candidate ability to perform position requirements. This interviewing technique plays into the strengths of job seekers who follow the preparation guidelines for the vignette strategy presented in Chapter 1. Vignettes are what these interviewers are looking for, and they are the perfect defense for an interviewer's assault with behavioral questions.

Résumé Probing

The same experienced interviewers might also painstakingly crawl their way through a résumé by asking job seekers to explain how they completed a certain task, why they did it, why they did not do it, why they left each company, why they joined each company, and many more questions that might provide some insight into competence level, intelligence, personality, and ability to perform the job functions. The responses might help the interviewer to form a 'chemistry' opinion. Job seekers must put up with this painstaking form of interrogation and respond to each question in clear, specific terms in a confident, enthusiastic, and positive manner. For each question, reach back into your experiences and make certain that by the end of the interview you provided vignettes covering all position requirements more than once.

The Inexperienced Interviewer

The other end of the spectrum for interviewer experience includes those who may be experts in their field but are novices at interviewing. This is exhibited by superficial questions, perhaps none being related to the open position. Inexperienced interviewers do not know how to determine if a job seeker satisfies the position needs. These interviews can be deceiving to job seekers who might falsely believe they hit it off well with the interviewer. *That was an easy interview— we didn't even talk about the job.* Wrong. These interviewers generally conclude that the job seeker is not qualified for the position because the job seeker did not talk about the job. The interviewer is always right.

Success with an inexperienced interviewer requires that job seekers be more forthcoming in presenting their accomplishments that relate to the position requirements. If the interviewer is still in the bonding mode after twenty or thirty minutes, then the job seeker must take the initiative. The first half hour could truly have resulted in developing a great relationship, but there is not much time remaining for job seekers to accomplish their mission: to convince the interviewer that you have performed all the requirements for the position and have a passion for doing them again.

Change the direction of the conversation in a very light, but direct way. I am really enjoying our conversation, Ann, but this is my only opportunity to convince you that I have the background your organization needs for the grant coordinator position. May I share some relevant experiences with you? Be polite and modest without being pushy and controlling. The inexperienced interviewer should be delighted that you are offering to share some experiences. Now, the interviewer can take some notes of substance and develop a more informative and positive opinion.

A Discouraging Interviewer

One of the interviewers might present negative aspects of the job for which you are interviewing. For example, the scope is too limited for someone with your experience, end users are so difficult to deal with that they caused the resignation of two incumbents, and budgets are usually cut in mid-year. The intent is usually to discourage you from taking the job offer if one is presented. This happened to Myra when she was interviewed by a consultant who will be replaced when the right candidate is found. The consultant could have used negative remarks to extend her lucrative contract or she might favor another candidate who will retain her for an on-going consulting relationship. Job seekers encountering this attitude should thank the interviewer for their candid assessment, express strong interest in the position and mention that you will consider each of the points if you should receive an offer. Do not be discouraged if you have this experience with only one of several interviewers. However, if your only interviewer acted in this manner, then you are likely not the interviewer's favorite candidate.

Illegal Questions

Federal and state laws such as the Americans With Disabilities Act (ADA) and the Civil Rights Act of 1964 (Title VII), amended in 1991, agency regulations, court rulings, and legislative decisions protect the privacy of personal information and ensure a level playing field for all individuals applying for a job. These laws make it illegal for interviewers to ask your age, weight, height, religion, national origin, sex, marital status, social organization memberships, and other personal information. Interviewers should ask questions that relate only to a candidate's ability to perform a particular job function.

There are occasions when an interviewer will ask a personal question and not be aware that it is inappropriate. Be prepared to respond. It will be a rare occurrence when the interviewer asks such a question in an offensive manner. In this instance you have every right to stand up and end the interview. However, if you want to win the interview game, you should leave your pride behind so that you can advance to the next level.

There is no reason to be nervous when asked a personal question as long as you prepare for these questions in advance of the interview. There are four approaches you can take during the interview.

1. *Answer the question.* This is the simplest approach. Where were you born? That question may have nothing to do with your ability to perform a job function, and the interviewer might just be curious. However, the company could have international business, and it might be viewed positively by the interviewer if you were raised in a foreign country.

2. *Do not answer the question.* You have the option of saying that you would rather not answer a question or that it has nothing to do with your ability to perform the job. End of interview. The interviewer could take this rebuff personally, view you as arrogant, and eliminate you from consideration. The reason for your elimination from consideration would be "other candidates more closely matched the position requirements."

3. *Determine the reason for the question.* Do you have young children? Although this is a personal question, it is possible that

the interviewer wants to know if children will prevent you from traveling or working late to perform your job. If the job requires travel, you can avoid mentioning your children by replying "I understand that the position requires extensive travel, and I would like you to know that I have no restrictions and would enjoy visiting company offices." If you are asked to describe your disability and are applying for a telemarketing position, you can reply that "I have five years of telemarketing experience and have used the telephone with exceptional results." That would be an excellent reply.

4. *Use humor in your answer.* Humor is a wonderful quality to insert once or twice in an interview. If you are in your late fifties and asked your age, you might reply that you have many years of playing tennis before being eligible for Social Security. Use humor to deflect questions in another direction.

Frequently Asked Questions

Responses to many questions should include previous experiences that illustrate your ability to perform the known position requirements. But what if the interviewer ignored your earlier request and did not divulge the skills required for the job? You must make your best assumptions based on what is known and reply with experiences you think are required for the position.

In most interview situations without a detailed list of required skills, job seekers should have asked for and been told position title, responsibilities, title of the person the position reports to, office location, extent of travel, and unusual aspects of the job. Hiring managers and HR professionals do not want to waste their valuable time interviewing candidates who might not accept an offer because of one or more of these factors.

To add substance to your responses, consider whatever is known about the job and turn up your listening skills to uncover other requirements. Questions asked by interviewers usually give away important position requirements or desired personality traits. For example, if asked "Describe your level of expertise in java," you might assume that one requirement for the winning candidate is hands-on technical skills in web development. If you are asked for your experience planning conferences, you can be sure that is one of the requirements for the job.

The following questions are asked frequently during interviews and each includes guidelines for a response. Be direct, maintain eye contact, smile occasionally, and use only positive remarks and congruent body language. The following are additional guidelines for answering interviewer questions:

➤ Do not provide a preamble, justification, or history leading to your answer.

➤ Provide one or two memorable vignettes with most answers.

➤ Ensure vignettes describe how you performed a particular function before, not how the company should perform it.

➤ Be modest and respectful, while responding confidently and with a friendly demeanor.

➤ Avoid the appearance of lecturing or being pompous or condescending.

1. What would you do in your first ninety days?

Response: Most interviewers are looking for someone who will commit to a measurable deliverable with a brief learning curve to get there. Hiring managers want a job seeker familiar with the company situation who has already developed ideas about improving it. An initial period of learning and planning is expected, but keep it to a minimum with a focus on contributing something significant to the organization in the first weeks or month. Be sure not to promise a business plan or vision on the first day of work. A lengthy planning period will also not be a favorable reply. The response should include one or more previous accomplishments that relate to the position requirements. Cite those as examples of what you might replicate early in the new job. Some job seekers are ambitious with their list of promised deliverables and that could be a double-edged sword. A long list might be the differentiator that results in a job offer, but failure to deliver could result in a three-month tenure, so be aggressive but realistic.

2. Why did you leave your last position?

Response: Interviewers label job seekers with negative remarks about a previous boss or company as complainers—not a good thing. Be honest, positive, and direct. A reference call might uncover the real reason you left. If you were fired, state so and do not be defensive or elaborate. Some acceptable and reasonable explanations include "my company was bought and the acquiring company let everyone go," "the company moved its offices to the Midwest and family commitments prevent me from relocating," "the company ran out of money," or "the recently hired CEO brought in a new management team."

3. What is your greatest strength?

Response: It is acceptable to be obvious with this answer. Describe vignettes that demonstrate your ability to satisfy one or two position requirements. If the position requires extensive experience developing financial models, then mention with pride that you have developed numerous complex models and thrived on the challenges each one presents. If you suspect but have not confirmed that another skill might be required, this is the opportunity to mention that skill with an accompanying vignette. If your response includes strengths not related to the needs of the company, then your candidacy could be in jeopardy.

4. What are some of your weaknesses?

Response: Provide only one weakness and hope that the interviewer is satisfied. The best format for this answer is to state a weakness and indicate what you are doing to correct it. The interviewer is waiting for you to volunteer a reason why you cannot perform the job for which you are interviewing. Do not fall into that trap. Your response should be totally unrelated to the job requirements and in a functional area outside the interviewer's area of expertise. For example, if you are applying for a human resources position and are being interviewed by a marketing person, pick a financial weakness. State that you only have a basic knowledge of accounting and are currently taking courses to improve that knowledge. Because accounting is not the interviewer's area of expertise, she might also acknowledge a weakness in the subject and you could establish a likeness leading to rapport. Another response could be that you had sometimes taken responsibility for more projects than you could handle. Follow up to say that subsequent experience has enabled you to do a better job of estimating and managing projects. Never describe an emotional weakness like a fear of flying or that you are seeing a psychologist to resolve a personal issue. That disclosure could result in a reject letter as soon as the interview is over.

5. How would your recent peers describe you?

Response: This question could have the same answer as the one about your strengths. Describe a different vignette that relates to a position requirement. There should be an additional point. Say that your peers would view you as very supportive; they trust you and can count on you for help. Convince the interviewer that you are a real team player and state that a number of peers would gladly serve as a reference.

6. Describe a project or accomplishment for which you are particularly proud.

Response: Refer to a project that is similar to one you might manage in the new position. Mention your interaction with senior management and members of other departments to demonstrate your ability to work in a matrix environment. You may also describe a relevant problem and how you solved it. You have discretion to mention any aspect of a project with which the interviewer would be impressed. An example might be how you applied a leadership skill like motivation, what you learned, and how the outcome helped the company. Be sure to describe how the company benefited from your action, not just you.

7. Why should we hire you?

Response: The answer an interviewer would like to hear is that you understand the requirements for the position by citing one or two as examples, you have accomplished those requirements at previous companies, and you are excited about doing them again for the interviewer's company. A reference to your familiarity with industry terminology, use of a company product, frequent visits to a company store, or some other connection would be excellent points to mention. An interviewer asked this question to a finalist for a customer service representative position. The candidate replied in a confident, energetic voice that she performed every responsibility in the job description during the previous four years working as a customer service rep. She stressed her telephone communication skills, service orientation, technical knowledge of the company's product line, and strong desire to work for the company. She got the job offer.

8. What have you been doing in the previous six months since you left your last job?

Response: To the extent the information is true, an ideal response for someone in this situation would be renewing and establishing relationships with industry contacts, networking and going on interviews, attending seminars, exercising, and increasing your participation in professional organizations. If you could say that you rejected an offer because it was not the right opportunity, then you would get a few extra game points. If you have been searching for almost a year, you should seek short-term consulting assignments so that you can include that in your response. Consulting assignments during a lengthy search demonstrate that you still have the skills to be successful in a full-time position.

9. You have been consulting on your own for the past year. How can we be sure you can make a successful transition to a line management position?

Response: Interviewers know that a transition from consulting to line management is very difficult. First of all, you should have a good reason for remaining a consultant for a year. Do not say that you needed the money. Rather, indicate that the assignments were taken to fill voids in your background and you now have substantially more experience going into your next full-time job. Describe consulting projects that enabled you to perform as a line manager recommending and delivering solutions, rather than simply advising a client and walking away. Draw as many parallels between consulting projects and job specifications, such as developing budgets, designing a web site, achieving sales quotas, and reporting progress to management. Implementation experience relevant to position requirements is what can convince interviewers that you are a doer and a transition to a corporate position would be an easy one.

10. What salary are you looking for?

Response: This is one question you should not answer. This is normally a fact-finding question asked in the first interview when salary was not known before scheduling the interview. The less risky answer is to state your current or most recent base salary, without mentioning a bonus, options, or other components of your previous package. Do not state what salary you desire. If forced to do so, say that you would expect an offer to be fair in light of the position responsibilities and do not mention a number. If that tactic does not work, then mention a range with the low end number being somewhat higher that your recent base. In salary negotiations, the first person to mention a desired amount is usually at the disadvantage. Providing a detailed list of perks without being asked often gives the wrong impression that all you want is money and not job satisfaction. Flexibility is a key attribute to exhibit when discussing salary in a first interview because there is another opportunity to negotiate salary after an offer is made.

11. Are you interviewing with other companies?

Response: Interviewers like to know how close a candidate might be to another job and to learn about the hiring needs of competing firms. If you are interviewing elsewhere, it is a good thing to acknowledge that you are in the early stages of interviews at other companies, but do not divulge company names. Interviewers may perceive that a person actively interviewing must have good qualities and should be given serious consideration. Such a response might also speed up the company's interview process to make sure that a hire/not-to-hire decision can be made before you accept another offer.

12. Why are you interested in our company?

Response: You are now given an opportunity to demonstrate your knowledge about the company uncovered in your research. Mention a few exciting things the company is doing, like introducing new products, reporting profitability, or starting a new venture. State the information in an upbeat voice as though you have known about this information for some time. Indicate that the company is one of the few you have selected to pursue because of its leading edge reputation. Your punch line should be that you are excited about applying your previous experience to help the company get to the next level.

13. Do you prefer to work alone or in teams?

Response: You should indicate that you have worked in both environments and provide brief vignettes for each. If you are certain the job requires you to work in a team environment, then say you prefer to be on a team, but have also worked successfully alone. If asked to pick one, the safer answer is being a part of a team unless you know the position you are seeking is clearly a one-person job.

14. Do you have any hobbies you would like to share with me?

Response: All work and no play makes for a boring employee, so you should have some outside interests to mention. Try to come up with your most unusual hobbies that will differentiate you from other candidates and make it easy for the interviewer to remember you. Taking an annual vacation to climb mountains, studying the martial arts, and sailing the Mediterranean are unusual. Interviewers are also looking for hobbies that complement and support the job requirements. For example, job seekers applying for a sales position should have hobbies that conjure up images of someone who is competitive and energetic.

15. Would you be willing to take a personality test?

Response: If you are asked this question, you can assume that a test is a requirement before an offer is extended. The safe answer is to agree to take the test. If the test is to be scheduled on another day, ask for the name of the test. Conduct research to learn the format of the test, its rules for completion, and possible outcomes. Chapter 6 discusses how you might move the results in your favor.

Neutralize the Age Issue

It is illegal to use a candidate's age as a factor in the hiring decision. Unfortunately, age can be a silent killer for an over fifty-year-old and an under thirty-year-old job seeker. Recruiters and human resource professionals can come close to age calculation based on key dates in a résumé. If one of these gatekeepers made the decision to interview you, there was likely little or no consideration given to age. Job seekers should therefore not blame age for a reject letter received after an interview. The two most common reasons for rejection of an old or young job seeker are failing to satisfy the position requirements or displaying the worst stereotyped characteristics of someone over age 50 or under age 30.

As interviewers take aim at job seekers during the question and answer period, they are assessing position requirements and personal attributes to determine if the job seeker can become an integral member of the company team. Job seekers have the power to neutralize the sensitive age issue.

Over Age 50

Too many job seekers over age 50 walk away from an interview saying: "They want a younger person." The real reasons are more likely that the job seeker lacked energy, wore old-fashioned clothing, spoke about accomplishments achieved thirty years ago, failed to demonstrate knowledge of new technology, exhibited dissatisfaction when introduced to a younger supervisor, bragged about a beautiful granddaughter, or just acted old. Avoid these factors and you should do well in an interview.

If there were a single quality that every hiring manager desires, it would be energy. Hiring managers want energetic employees with stamina to survive long days and weekends to get the job done. Job seekers must create the perception of being physically fit, alert, and active. A powerful age neutralizer is to mention that you have been attending a spinning class with an aggressive instructor, running ten miles every few days, or playing in a weekly basketball game. Job seekers at every age, especially over fifty, should give a rigorous activity serious consideration for their personal well-being and interview game points. If you are not already participating, begin an activity before an important interview and you can honestly say that you have started. Interviewers will undoubtedly perceive that you have the stamina of someone ten years younger. There should also be "energy" vignettes waiting to be played. One example would be to describe projects that required long days and extensive travel.

Clothing and appearance can make men and women look younger with a conservative yet stylish look. Women should wear a modern hairstyle and men should know that greasy hair formulas are no longer in fashion. Go to a hair stylist a week before the interview and ask for a conservative, young looking, neatly trimmed look. Some gray hair could look distinguished, and a good dye for some might help to remake your image and attitude. Dress sharply. If you are overweight, take advantage of being out of work by going on a diet and entering an exercise program. Feel good about yourself and your looks before going on interviews. After taking special care to look sharp, do not bring that twenty-year-old, beat-up attaché case. Make sure the contents of anything you bring are neatly stacked and do not fly all over the room when opened. An extreme step for a small number of candidates might be to consider plastic surgery for droopy eyelids or bags under the eyes.

A trap that many over fifty job seekers fall into is that they focus on what they did many, many years ago, rather than being proud of what they are currently doing or plan to do. The recent ten years of experience are the relevant years being evaluated by prospective employers and what you accomplished in the recent five years will likely get you the next job. If you really believe that something you did more than twenty years ago will help your candidacy, then describe the accomplishment without stating when you did it. When finished, move off the topic quickly to prevent the interviewer from asking when it happened.

If a position requires ten years of travel industry experience and you have thirty years, do not try to convince the interviewer that you are three times more qualified than everyone else. That will raise the overqualified flag, especially if you reinforce what the interviewer can determine from the résumé. Emphasize that your accomplishments in the recent ten years are right on target with the company's travel industry requirements.

Flexibility is an excellent attribute of youth—your competition. If you tell an interviewer I did it that way at my previous company, you might leave the impression that you will do it no other way. A better comment would be to state that you performed a similar function at your previous company and continuously improved the process. Flexibility also comes into play when discussing salary. A younger person might say that 5 percent to 10 percent less than the last job would be acceptable after being convinced there is a budget ceiling because they have confidence that performance will be rewarded. Older workers need to demonstrate the same flexibility and confidence. There is also a perception that older workers are not technically savvy. Break that perception by describing projects in which you interfaced heavily with web developers and systems staff and that you never leave home without a Palm Pilot or laptop computer.

Another consideration as you approach sixty is to realize that companies will not hire you for succession planning to replace your boss. You should anticipate that by offering your skills on a full-time or an interim basis. As preparation for an interview try to identify company projects that might require three, six, or more months of your time to complete. During the interview you can weave your way to discussing those projects and offering your services on a project-by-project basis. This could be a win-win situation that might lead to a full-time position. Finally, older candidates should know popular songs, singers, musicians, artists, and actors favored by younger generations, and one or two names should be mentioned in casual conversation as your favorites.

Under Age 30

This group does not have as many barriers to go through as its counterpart at the other end of the calendar. Recent graduates in their twenties may have a hard time getting a management position in an established company where the average age is in the forties or higher. Maturity, conservative dress, and previous experience managing projects will go a long way. Performing a leadership role in professional organizations and giving presentations at industry conferences project a very knowledgeable and mature image.

The most important preparation that will pave the way for a successful interview is to describe vignettes that convey years of experience related to position requirements. These vignettes can be pulled from work accomplishments, outside professional activities, travel, summer projects, and unusual hobbies. Members in this age group can also cite some relevant and meaningful activities performed while in college or graduate school, since that would be less than ten years earlier. Avoid inappropriate language or slang. For example, do not use "you know," "cool," "totally," or similar expressions. These terms can be annoying to older interviewers. If you have a high-pitched voice, practice bringing it down an octave or two.

During times of high unemployment, older workers will be competing for jobs normally taken by younger workers. Know perceived weaknesses of older workers and impress interviewers by being alert, flexible, enthusiastic, energetic, and well prepared. Demonstrate a positive, upbeat attitude with a willingness to do whatever it takes.

Big Company Small

In recent years, there has been an increase in hiring by small and mid-size companies. Job seekers have not missed this opportunity. The thrust of questions asked by small company hiring managers focuses not only on the ability of job seekers to perform the position requirements but also to adjust to a small company environment. Small company executives know that job seekers coming from Fortune 1000 companies will experience culture shock and must be able to adapt to the drastic changes in office support, decision making, and speed of project completion.

The classification 'small company' is a relative term. If a job seeker has spent a career with companies generating billions of dollars in revenue, then a move to a company with $100 million would be going to a small company. Anyone interviewing with a start-up company by definition is going to a smaller company. Job seekers with prior large company experience must overcome perceptions, some real and some stereotyped, held by hiring managers at small companies. In general, convey as much likeness as possible between your large corporate environment and a small company to convince interviewers that you know how to get things done in a small company. The following are the common perceptions and how they can be addressed during an interview.

Large Staff

When preparing for an interview in a small company, find out very discretely how many staff are in the company and how many will report to you. Do not let this be the first question or it might be your last question. Select projects you led in previous companies that had a similar number of staff and some that had no staff reporting to you.

Describe relevant vignettes and mention the pride you took in preparing your own reports, PowerPoint presentations, and spreadsheets to the extent that you did. Describe the matrix organization in which you obtained support of staff from other departments even though no one reported to you. Limit your vignettes to projects and accomplishments that were achieved on small projects, in entrepreneurial ventures, or divisions of larger organizations similar in size to the small company environment. Describe only situations where you worked in environments similar in size and scope to the company you are interviewing with.

Significant Financial Resources

Small company hiring managers almost always think job seekers from large companies have deep pockets and large budgets when managing projects. Large company job seekers know that is not always true. There are many projects that are run on a shoestring and that point must be conveyed during an interview with a small company manager. A business development director at a Fortune 500 company was given the assignment to enter into a marketing alliance with another company and was given a budget of $20,000, not $200,000 or $2 million. That was truly a challenge, but the resourceful director used the high profile project to obtain equipment donations and attract volunteers from other departments that wanted to gain notoriety from participating in the important project. Creative use of limited resources will impress interviewers.

Management by Committee

Decision making in large companies involves following written procedures and a considerable amount of time that is necessary to reach consensus among the many department heads and key staff. Not so in small companies. Job seekers should describe vignettes that demonstrate interaction with senior management resulting in decisions to approve or disapprove proposed projects. In small companies, a staff member walks into the president's office with an idea and the decision might be made immediately to move forward. Another president might ask the staff member to make the recommendation at the next staff meeting and the decision might be made at that time. You should convince interviewers that you previously experienced rapid decision making similar to that which occurs often in small companies.

Project Management

Projects at large companies tend to take longer than projects at smaller companies, usually because of the larger scope. As a result, small company hiring managers are concerned that job seekers from large companies will not have a sense of urgency that is required in smaller companies. Job seekers must rely on vignettes to convince interviewers that bonus, reputation, and job were at stake, and long days and weekends were devoted to completing projects on time and within budget.

Frequent Job Changes

If you had frequent job changes in the past five years, then you will certainly be asked to explain why you left each company after a short tenure. Recruiting an employee is very costly for any company, especially small ones with less money. Additional probing for job changers will take place to ensure that these individuals have valid and reasonable explanations for leaving each company. If you have changed jobs frequently and were still invited for an interview, there must be some accomplishments and skills listed in your résumé that attracted attention. Determine these desired skills and play the right vignettes to convince interviewers they made the right decision to interview you.

The reasons you left each company should be presented with a brief explanation in a matter-of-fact, confident tone. Do not provide an excuse for departing. Instead, state a valid business reason for your career change. If your candidacy reaches the final stage of interviews and an offer is imminent, you can be assured that reference checking will probe for the reasons why you left each company in recent years. Any new employer would want to make certain that they are not the next stop in a series of short visits.

Economic news can be a reason for job changers in the late 1990s and early 2000s. The dotcom era of that time is widely known for luring employees from large corporations to start-up ventures. Companies grew quickly with fresh capital resulting in a large number of employees who were within the grasp of wealth with stock options. Unfortunately, the newfound capital was burned at an alarming rate causing large numbers of job losses and shrinking values for stock options. Many of these displaced employees wanted to roll the dice more than once and went from one dotcom to another, only to watch each one fade away or get bought—resulting in yet another job loss. This period of job frenzy should be understood by a reasonable prospective employer.

One possible advantage of frequent job changes is that you should have learned new skills during each short stint. Be certain to inform interviewers of relevant skills learned. One of these valuable experiences could have been a total immersion in an entrepreneurial environment with its rapid-fire decision-making capability in a flat organization, very few subordinates, and lean budgets where you obtained a great appreciation for what teamwork and "hands-on" really mean. Personal networks of some executives and middle managers could have been expanded to include venture capitalists, investment bankers, and industry executives. Focus on what was learned and not the emotional roller coaster going from job to job.

Changing Industries

Getting a job in another industry requires a significant amount of research into the practices, regulations, major companies, products, and other aspects unique to the new industry. It can be done. Consultants do this all the time before tackling a new assignment. The successful mind-set that will facilitate the change is to identify a likeness to an industry employee in as many ways as possible. Incorporate some exposure or experience related to the new industry into your elevator speech. Rewrite your résumé to remove, or make generic, all terms unique to your previous industry experience and incorporate in any way possible reference to the new industry using its terminology.

A key ingredient to make the switch is a long-term passion for the industry that surfaces in a hobby, frequent attendance at industry conferences, and volunteer work performed over the years. Before going on company interviews in a new industry, your research should enable you to carry on a conversation about the new industry's politics, recent news items, high profile executives, unusual company activities, and innovative product offerings. You must create the perception that you are very knowledgeable in the industry even though your résumé does not reflect extensive experience.

Do not use terminology from your previous industry during the interview, otherwise, the interviewer will conclude that you will not be able to adapt to the new industry. Rather, you should use the new industry terminology to the best of your ability as if you were already working in that industry. You can indicate, to the extent that it is true, that you have always been interested in the interviewer's industry, subscribe to industry publications, have many industry contacts, and have transferable skills for which new industry friends ask advice. Your research on the Internet and with networking contacts should identify skills from your functional discipline (e.g., finance, marketing, human resources, sales, administrative, engineering, etc.) that apply to the industry in which you are trying to break into. Describe those skills to the interviewer while being careful not to refer to your current industry. Demonstrate that you have an excitement about participating in the growth of a company in the new industry.

Too many job seekers make statements in interviews like, "My previous industry skills can be transferred to your industry." That is presumptuous. Job seekers have no credibility when they say that previous skills can be transferred to another industry. Interviewers need to be convinced and that statement must be supported by specific experience. For example, Kyomi was an accounting manager for a consumer goods company manufacturing tooth paste and she was interviewing for an accounting position in the chemical industry. During her interview, she described how she maintained accounting records for the end product, and, after a few months, her supervisor asked her to keep track of costs for the chemical components of the toothpaste. She mentioned the names of some chemical compounds and impressed her interviewers.

Long-Term Unemployment

Recruiters and HR professionals may have a negative bias against job seekers who are out of work for an extended period, say more than nine months. There is the perception, albeit often incorrect, that currently employed and recently unemployed job seekers are more capable and more desired by hiring managers than job seekers who have been involved in a prolonged search. If you are in this situation, you must convince interviewers that you have not been home watching television all that time. Mention courses you have taken, classes you have taught, offers you may have turned down, and relevant consulting assignments regardless of how brief they might have been or if they were performed pro bono.

During an interview and in everyday conversation you must always have a positive attitude and be "on" at all times. Individuals with upbeat personalities are a pleasure to be around. However, this important positive façade becomes difficult to maintain when the search drags on for many months, and interviewers are the first to make that observation. Job seekers in a prolonged transition must continuously find ways to reinvigorate and re-energize their search to hide their underlying feelings. The following three suggestions are applicable to recent graduates and senior executives:

➤ *Attend networking, professional, and social events.* These gatherings are where potential employers, sources of information, and business contacts are found.

➤ *Identify individuals with positive, upbeat personalities, and make plans to be with them often.* Attitude can be contagious and you will be a better player if you are surrounded by people who always see the glass more than half full.

➤ *Volunteer your time with not-for-profit organizations.* Volunteering provides an opportunity to demonstrate your professional skills in a nonthreatening setting. Other volunteers are usually employed or the spouse of an employed person. Your accomplishments and contributions would be recognized by the organization and observed by the many volunteers with whom you will be working. Unexpected rewards are often a benefit in these situations.

Overqualified

Hearing an interviewer tell you that you are overqualified need not be the end of an interview. One use of this unwelcome term might be as a euphemism for *There is no chemistry* or *Your personality is not acceptable in our environment.* The interviewer has no reason to reject your candidacy based on your ability to satisfy the position requirements. Job seekers have little recourse to overcome this type of rejection.

The second and more common use of the overqualified accusation is the unspoken view that you are too old, your salary is too high, and/or the work is too menial based on your previous experience and title. This use of the term should be assumed and an attempt made to convince interviewers otherwise. Taking steps to overcome the age issue was previously addressed. The concerns about having a high salary and performing low level tasks could be confronted head-on. Respond that you know your previous salary was higher than what is budgeted for this position, and you will be flexible on that issue. Inform the interviewer how closely you satisfy the position requirements, how excited you are to work in a company at the leading edge of their industry, and how much value you can add to the company's growth. State one or two examples of how you can add value. Continue the rebuttal by acknowledging you previously performed some of the work in earlier jobs, you enjoyed doing so, and received considerable praise. State that you recognize the position is at a level lower than you recently held, however, you have subsequently developed many ways to increase productivity and achieve a higher standard of quality.

The Interview Game Continues

Susan just made her first impression, established rapport, and put her interview strategy in motion during her meeting with Scott Gilbert, the VP-HR. It took ten minutes. She determined the skills Scott is looking for and she is prepared for the onslaught of questions that consumes the middle of an interview. In his role as VP-HR, Scott's evaluation of Susan is broader than making sure she can perform the position requirements. Soft skills are equally important to Scott. He is the ombudsman for the entire staff and has direct responsibility to the president. Scott must ascertain that Susan will be a welcomed team player with her peers across the company, the senior management team, and the administrative support staff. Can Scott trust Susan to represent the company at internal meetings and at industry conferences, can she roll her sleeves up and perform some detailed analysis when needed, will she help others without getting any credit? These are some of the soft qualities Scott must evaluate.

Susan's objective is to create real images and positive perceptions to demonstrate her ability to satisfy the position requirements and appropriate personal qualities. This is the approach needed to get a return invitation for another round of interviews.

Susan takes three deep breaths, sits upright, leans a bit forward, and listens attentively for Scott to ask the leading question to this part of the interview. She knows Scott will be assessing her ability to perform the required job functions and her level of interest in both the job and the company. He will also be observing her personality under the stress of the interview.

Susan focuses on demonstrating her soft skills. These skills relate to personality, demeanor, attitude, energy, conscientiousness, and other factors contributing to being liked by an interviewer and creating a good chemistry. Excellent soft skills often overcome any built-in negative feeling of an interviewer. She conducts the interview with a very positive, upbeat, attitude; smiles frequently; and demonstrates pent-up energy. Susan repeats in her mind the two position requirements confirmed by the VP-HR:

1. To increase the magazine subscription base.

2. To apply direct marketing techniques.

Susan's strategy for the remainder of the interview is to describe the vignettes that demonstrate how she performed the two position requirements. This becomes a recurring theme for Susan. Her vignettes are listed under the first page of her notepad and she is prepared to use them as Scott begins to ask his questions.

Scott: Describe how you recently impressed your supervisor.

Susan: My immediate supervisor would make an excellent reference. My marketing efforts directly resulted in **increasing the number of subscribers** 20 percent each year. A second impressive feat that my supervisor would mention is the marketing alliance I initiated, negotiated, and implemented with ANS Publications. Our content is complementary and our audience has a similar demographic. The agreement was for each company to send a promotional announcement to the other company's subscribers, and the result was **25,000 new subscribers** for us last year.

Scott: How did you achieve such a high growth rate each year?

Susan: There are two approaches that largely account for that growth. First, I entered into two other alliances similar to what I just described and with comparable results. Second, an even greater success story was achieved through the **use of direct marketing techniques**. I used a combination of traditional direct marketing with hard copy promotion material and e-mail promotions sent to a purchased list of targeted recipients. I personally kept track of the results of each marketing approach and focused on continuous improvement to achieve the growth we did.

Scott: Why did you join your current firm three years ago?

Susan: Well, at that time the Internet was beginning to be used as a direct marketing tool and I wanted to broaden my experience in that area. After completing three years at the company, I have spoken at two industry conferences as **an authority on the use of e-mail as a direct marketing tool.**

Scott: What you are you really good at?

Susan: One of my key strengths is the ability to assess a situation and determine the best approach for improvement. For example, at least twice annually, I **review the number of new subscribers**, the number of cancellations, the reasons for cancellations, the results of previous marketing campaigns, and other statistics. I conduct a brief but thorough assessment to **determine the direct marketing techniques** that will be required to sustain our growth and then I set in motion steps to implement those techniques.

Scott: Please describe your perspective on the industry.

Susan: This industry is on the path of high growth. One of your biggest competitors, XLM Publications located ten miles away, just bought a small industry player and should be watched carefully. Your recent marketing alliance with CPT Publications can be a significant contributor to your revenue stream.

Susan answered most of Scott's questions with words taken from the two position requirements. She also mentioned some interesting knowledge she obtained about a competitor and a recent alliance observed in a press release. Susan intentionally added that the large competitor, XLM Publications, is located ten miles away. That sends a clear message to Scott that if he believes Susan is a good candidate, he better speed up the interview process, otherwise, he might lose her to the competition. Scott listened to Susan's accomplishments in the form of vignettes that relate to the position requirements. If she can refer to those requirements in most responses for the remaining questions, Scott should soon reach the opinion that Susan has done what his company needs. Susan is a natural when it comes to the soft skills and she proceeds to impress Scott on all fronts.

Immediately after responding to the last question about her industry knowledge, Susan asks Scott a question, "Do you anticipate entering into any alliances or joint ventures in the coming year?" If the questions are completely mono-directional, the interviewer may think the job seeker has little interest. It is appropriate and recommended to insert one or two questions of your own. This particular question was intended to reinforce Susan's experience in forming alliances. If Scott replies that his company plans some activity in that area, Susan has made yet another winning move.

Job seekers should respond to the barrage of interview questions in a way that impresses the interviewer with both qualifications and personality. Uncover each interviewer's skill requirements early in the interview. If they cannot be identified, then job seekers must surface one or more needs during the question and answer period or take a best guess to identify those needs. You must convince interviewers that key skills were applied at previous companies and that you are excited about performing them again.

The interview clock shows that ten minutes remain.

Chapter 4 | End with a Lasting Impression:
Any Interviewer, Any Venue

The first interview is almost over. You now have the opportunity to leave a lasting and favorable impression or to salvage a session that may not have gone well. The signal for this moment is when the interviewer asks, "Do you have any questions?" Your answer is almost as important as the response to the "tell me about yourself" request. The interviewer is in no mood to restart the interview; so do not pull out your list of twenty questions. You are still in selling mode and the goal of every word in these last few minutes is to keep your candidacy alive.

The Beginning of the End

Susan's interview has finally reached this point. When she is asked the trigger question by Scott, the VP-HR, she is primed to inject renewed energy into the discussion so that she can finish on an upbeat and positive note. Susan provides the following response:

> Thank you for asking. I am really excited about the position and the possibility of becoming a part of your team. You have given me a clear description of the position responsibilities, and I have one question. Since this is the only opportunity for me to present my experience and qualifications, do you have any questions or areas in my background that you would like me to clarify?

The first thing Susan did was to verbalize a strong desire for the position. Job seekers should never assume interviewers know how they feel. Candidate interest is always an evaluation factor, and recruiters, human resource professionals, and hiring managers do not

75

want to waste time with lukewarm candidates. Express that interest with excitement and sincerity.

Susan also preempted a concern of many interviewers by stating she understands the position requirements. If no questions are asked, interviewers often wonder whether job seekers know what the job entails, and the risk of a mismatch enters the interviewer's mind. Susan succeeds in removing any doubt about this issue.

Her question can possibly salvage an unsuccessful interview. The interviewer has two possible responses. The first is to say I have everything I need and we will follow-up in a week or so. This response is not at all helpful and the job seeker must hope for the best. The second option is for interviewers to be more forthcoming and provide a direct and honest answer, to a degree. For instance, the interviewer might identify a previously unmentioned position requirement with which the job seeker appears to have minimal experience. Thus, "Susan, you do not seem to have experience working with an ad agency." In this situation, Susan has a final chance to save the day by extracting an unused vignette.

Scott stands to signal the end of the interview and thanks Susan for meeting with him. She also stands, thanks Scott for taking the time to meet with her and asks when she can expect to hear from him. He tells her within two weeks. Susan extends her hand, reminiscent of the first impression moment, with full smile, firm handshake, direct eye contact, and, with a confident voice, she says that she looks forward to hearing from him. As she leaves the office, Susan makes it a point to bid farewell to the receptionist and remarks that she hopes they can meet again.

You Want to Know My Salary?

The last thing parents will tell their children is the amount of money they take home each week. Divulging the amount is often compared to sharing an embarrassing health problem with a physician. Yet, executive recruiters and human resources executives do not hesitate to request your current and recent compensation, including every last perk. Be prepared for this question at the end of the interview, but never initiate this discussion topic. The tone of your reply can kill your candidacy.

Advance knowledge of the salary range budgeted for the position can help you formulate a winning answer to the salary question. Compensation components for most jobs include an hourly rate or annual base salary plus performance bonus. Sales positions normally discuss compensation in terms of total income, which includes base salary plus expected commission if target sales are achieved. Senior executive pay packages may include deferred compensation, a car allowance, stock options, a percent of company ownership, club memberships, use of company jet, and other perks. Be prepared to provide the list only if requested to do so.

The winning approach to the salary request in the first interview is to convey the appearance of being flexible on the issue. If you should receive an offer at the end of the game, you will have the opportunity to negotiate as firmly as you wish when you are in a position of strength.

The Simple Answer

If you are reasonably certain that the company budgeted a salary higher than your most recent earnings, you should state in a matter-of-fact tone your current or most recent hourly rate or base salary, the percent of performance bonus or amount of commission received, and other compensation components you believe are significant. The manner in which you state your compensation should leave the impression that you merely replied to the question and the response was not a demand that the company meet or exceed that amount. The concern job seekers should have when describing their salary is the risk of being perceived as caring more about money than company and position.

The Complex Answer

If you are reasonably certain that the base budgeted for the position is less than you were earning, the interview could reach an untimely conclusion. Depending on how much the company is willing to pay, the best you can hope for when negotiating after you receive an offer is for the company to match your current or recent base. When asked for your compensation in this situation, there are two options that can save your candidacy if you have flexibility on this important issue and want to win the game. These options should also be successful if you are not sure of the targeted salary.

1. *State your recent hourly rate or base salary and mention that you also receive a bonus or commission, but do not specify that amount.* Observe the interviewer's reaction. If the company's budgeted base is dramatically lower than yours, the interviewer might tell you so and say that there is no way the two of you can ever get together on salary. Your reply to that gloomy prospect is to ask what their targeted base is. If you are willing to take a cut in salary for the position, then, without appearing desperate, you should convincingly state that the close match with your skills and the experience you could gain make the lower salary acceptable. If company interviewers are impressed with your credentials, flexibility on both sides could lead to a successful compromise.

2. *Provide the interviewer with your base salary for the most recent three jobs if you believe your salary in one or two of these previous jobs was at or below the budgeted number.* For example, suppose the company is budgeting $60,000 for the position and the salaries in your recent three positions within the past five years were $70,000, $60,000, and $55,000. If you state the three salaries in response to a request for your recent salary, interviewers might make the assumption that you will accept a lower salary, a discussion could be averted, and you could still be in the game.

Request for References

A job seeker without a reference is a job seeker without a job. References are among the most valuable assets of any job seeker. They must be protected and not shared until absolutely necessary. A small percent of job seeker résumés includes a list of three, four, or five references on the last page. Unscrupulous recipients of your résumé could initiate unwanted sales calls to references and it will not be long before a reference makes the connection to you. That could result in an embarrassing reference loss.

Normal protocol is for references to be requested only from two or three finalist candidates at the end of the interview process. However, some HR professionals are requesting references in the first interview. The rationale for these early requests is to avoid entering into a lengthy interview process should one or two references send out negative signals about a job seeker.

If job seekers are asked to provide references, at any time in the process, it is reasonable to ask HR staff and recruiters when and which ones they will call. Before you provide anyone with the name of a reference, you must alert the reference to a possible call. In response to a request for a few references, reply that you will ensure that they are available and then provide the interviewer with contact information. Protecting and preparing your references are presented in Chapter 6.

Document the Interview

During the dream days of the dotcom era at the turn of the twenty-first century, hiring was fast and furious. In the early 2000s with unemployment rising and companies believing they had an ample supply of candidates to find the "perfect" match, the interview process dragged on for three, four, or five months. Due to the potentially lengthy elapsed time between interviews, it is critical for job seekers to document as much about each interview as possible. At the second and subsequent interviews, the best perception is created when job seekers show total recall about what took place at the previous interview, as if it occurred the previous day.

Susan feels like she is walking on air when she exits the building and heads straight to a quiet place away from the vicinity of the company. This could be a commuter train, a public library, or your home if the distance is not too far. She begins recording interview details that can be used to her advantage during the second and subsequent interviews discussed in Chapter 5.

➣ Date and time of the interview. The weather should be noted if it were unusual because it could be a subsequent conversation topic.

➣ Name, address, title, telephone, e-mail of everyone met, including receptionists and company staff met in the building.

➣ Names, titles, and organizational relationships of other employees mentioned by interviewers. Build an organization chart with information offered by each interviewer or obtained from listening.

➣ Position requirements with similarities and differences stated by each interviewer to identify their individual areas of interest.

➣ Questions asked by each interviewer that provide insight into their concerns, the vignettes you played, and new position requirements identified.

➣ Your impressions of each interviewer. Indicate if friendly and approachable, serious or has a sense of humor, personal interests, and if you established a good rapport that would enable you to contact this person at a future time.

➣ A unique aspect of each interviewer that can be referred to in future conversations, like an interesting hobby, foreign language ability, or a recent trip.

➣ Commonality, or likeness, between you and each interviewer that led or could lead to rapport.

➣ Comments or inferences about other candidates (e.g., strengths, weaknesses, companies or industries worked, etc.) which can be used to your advantage in the next interview.

➣ Information or work product an interviewer requested or had a need for.

➣ Areas that require additional preparation if invited for another interview.

Thank-You Note

A well-written thank-you note can have a positive affect on one's candidacy. Despite this, many job seekers do not write one. Prepare a note—it just might save your candidacy. Experienced job seekers take an hour or more to prepare a brief, tailored thank-you note for each interviewer. But beware: a poorly written note with just one spelling error will almost certainly kill a good interview. Take your time, be clear, to the point, and use spelling and grammar check. The contents denote your social and communications skills.

The purpose of the note, apart from thanking the interviewer for taking time to meet with you, is to stand out from the crowd and to strengthen your candidacy. Sample notes appear in Exhibit 4-1. Examples of a conservative approach and contents for an effective thank-you note follow:

➤ Thank the interviewer for taking the time to meet with you.

➤ Reiterate your interest and excitement in the position and the company.

➤ Help the interviewer to remember you by identifying a personal connection made during the interview.

➤ Remind the interviewer of one or two key strengths you believe are relevant and likely not possessed by competing candidates. This should be very brief and is optional. A lengthy repetition of your résumé and what was discussed during the interview could be viewed negatively.

➤ Include a key experience or accomplishment you forgot to mention if you believe that it is relevant to the position requirements.

➤ Keep the note brief and less than half a page.

➤ Attach personal or professional information requested by an interviewer or volunteered by you during the interview. Material can include a favorite restaurant, an extract of a report you previously prepared, or other supporting information.

A separate note should be sent to each person met. If for some reason, all names or contact information were not obtained, send the note to a key person whose contact information you know, and ask that person to pass along your appreciation to the other members of the interview team.

(text continues on page 87)

EXHIBIT 4-1 Sample Thank-You Notes

The use of a first name in the salutation is a personal decision based on the rapport established during the interview. The subject could simply be "thank-you."

Sample Note 1

Dear Mr. Smith:

Thanks, again, for taking the time to discuss the sales management opportunity at The West Coast Corporation. I came away from our meeting energized with the possibility of applying my experience and contacts in the financial and professional services sectors. Attached is a sales commission plan I prepared a few years ago, confidential information removed, that I think you will find helpful as you begin to hire your sales staff. Be assured that I'll rearrange my schedule to be available for another meeting at your convenience.

Best regards,

Marita

Sample Note 2

Dear Tina:

Thanks for meeting with me today during your busy schedule. I appreciated and enjoyed our discussion. My interest and excitement about the web development position at EastCoast.com grows with each person I meet in the interview process. I would like very much to apply my technology experience as a member of your team. Looking forward to the next step! Thanks, again.

Sincerely,

Bill

(continues)

EXHIBIT 4-1 (continued)

Sample Note 3

Dear Christine:

Thank you for meeting with me on such short notice and describing your needs at the Fast Telecom Company. The challenges you mentioned for the VP-HR position, including staff retention, job satisfaction, employee relations and counseling, and strategic planning with possible expansion internationally are areas of personal interest and in which I have hands-on experience. At my previous company, I developed a reputation as an excellent employee ombudsman and senior management team resource. Hope to hear from you soon.

Sincerely,

Larry

Sample Note 4

> Dear Sean:
>
> I know how busy you are and I would like to thank you for taking the time to meet with me today. Please extend my appreciation to Greg and Beth. Since our discussion, I have gotten more excited about the possibility of becoming part of the TRN team. It really is a small world with both of us staying at the same farmhouse in Tuscany within a week of each other. I look forward to hearing from you soon.
>
> Sincerely,
>
> Alex

Interviewer Reply

> It was a pleasure meeting with you as well. Greg and Beth were both very impressed with your credentials. Our Human Resources Director, Stephanie, will contact you shortly to discuss next steps.

(continues)

EXHIBIT 4-1 *(continued)*

Sample Note 5

Dear Bob:

Thank you very much for taking the time to describe the internet security position. It was a pleasure meeting you, and I am very excited about the prospect of leading the team to reinvigorate an already highly successful product line. I look forward to seeing you again and meeting the rest of the management team.

Sincerely,

Stu

Thank-you notes should be sent within one day after the interview to achieve maximum effectiveness. Timely and well-written notes may influence the decision to invite a job seeker back for another round of interviews and they are expected by interviewers. A delay in receiving one can gnaw at an interviewer. Some job seekers prefer to send a handwritten note to make it more personal, even though it may take three to five days to reach the recipient. In today's environment, speed is critical and that makes e-mail the fastest and most effective means of delivery. If you received the e-mail address of an interviewer, send the note via e-mail. If your interview was on a Friday, a paper note could be acceptable if it arrives by Monday.

If you are risk averse or believe that you did well during your interview, then remain in conservative mode. Susan believed that she established a great rapport with Scott and conveyed with convincing vignettes that she possessed the required experience for the position. Based on that assumption, she sent a friendly thank-you note, including a reminder of the Paris connection and a clear statement of excitement.

A Risky Thank-You

There is another approach that falls into the high-risk, high-reward category. If the hiring manager described a major problem, such as a need to develop a business plan or to train a project team, you may wish to take the time and attach a draft solution with your thank-you note. Let's say the hiring manager complained about a business problem; you can attach a description of the problem as you understood it and provide a well-thought-out approach to its solution. Your proposed solution would have additional credibility if you can say you applied a similar solution to a similar problem in a previous job. In response to the need for a business plan, you can develop a detailed outline of the plan's contents with enough substance to impress the reader. Again, cite previous experience preparing similar plans. If the hiring manager mentioned the need for expertise in developing a complex financial spreadsheet, you can attach an example of one you completed for an important project being sure to remove confidential information. The risk of attaching these types of documents is that you could be viewed as presumptuous or you could be way off the mark on your recommendations. However, very few job seekers submit attachments to a thank-you note and an impressive document that comes close to the expectations of an interviewer could catapult you to the top of the candidate list. If you are generally a risk taker or if you believe that your interview did not go well, this approach could give you a second chance.

Waiting for Feedback

Waiting to find out the results of an interview is one of the worst frustrations experienced by job seekers. Do not expect the ideal feedback loop after an interview. Information hand-off regarding the status of your candidacy from client (to recruiter, if one is involved) to you may take days, weeks, or sometimes months. The bottleneck can be the company. One reason an HR professional might not send a reject letter and end the misery could be that the search is continuing for the "perfect" candidate. When none is found some months hence, the company's head of recruiting wants the ability to reopen discussions with earlier candidates. That is no excuse. The company should send candidates a status letter regardless of the situation.

Recruiters can be your best friends when they promote your candidacy with a client; but they can avoid your repeated calls when you are not the preferred candidate. Lack of feedback from a recruiter might be due to other candidates going back for multiple interviews and the recruiter does not wish to share the bad news. She might be using you as backup if top candidates get eliminated and does not want you to lose interest in the client opportunity. Another reason for no feedback could be that you were submitted to a client by a recruiter who never learned the proper protocol of keeping candidates up-to-date.

Fear of rejection and the accompanying anxiety are common concerns after an interview. The best way to suppress those feelings is to take control and bring the waiting period to a conclusion as quickly as possible. At the same time, increase the pace of networking, attend seminars, and perform other job search activities to divert your focus from waiting for a gatekeeper's call.

At the end of each interview, you should ask the HR manager when feedback might be expected, and you should inform the recruiter so you can both be frustrated. If there is no recruiter, you will wait alone. The day after the news is due, send an e-mail and/or call the recruiter or company recruiting manager to ask for the status of your candidacy. If the recruiter ignores your repeated calls, then you should consider sending a nonintrusive e-mail to the human resources contact only if you established a rapport. The e-mail message should indicate that you have not heard from the recruiter, assuming there is one, and you are still very interested in the opportunity. Add that you would appreciate an update on the timing of the next step in the interview process. If you are fortunate to have received an offer from another company during this waiting period, Chapter 6 describes how to deal with this exciting prospect. Another means to determine interview status is to e-mail a company interviewer with whom you established rapport, expressing your understanding that the person may not be in a position to give you an answer. A final approach might be to identify a competing candidate and call that individual with an offer to share information. This tactic is discussed in Chapter 5.

Other First-Time Interviewers

Susan's first interview included only the VP-HR, a powerful gatekeeper. Her approach should be used as a primer for all first-time interviews. Recruiters, hiring managers, senior management, peers, and other employees can all be players in the first round of interviews. Do not assume everyone agrees on the same position requirements. Each person has a different agenda with unique needs, depending on their perspective and position in the company. Your job is to uncover those needs and to convince each interviewer you have satisfied them before and are capable of repeating previous successes. Again, establishing a rapport with every interviewer is the path to a successful interview. Identify areas of likeness between you and each interviewer to achieve the required level of rapport.

Executive Recruiters

Executive recruiters (a.k.a. headhunters) are hired by their client companies to find qualified individuals for all levels of positions and functional skills. Recruiters fall into two general classifications: contingency and retained. Some recruiters perform both types of searches. Each serves as a gatekeeper for their clients by interviewing job seekers and forwarding only résumés of capable candidates.

Contingency recruiting firms are paid a fee for their service only after a job seeker submitted to a client company accepts an offer and begins to work. Hiring companies may use one or more contingency firms to fill a position. For a company using several recruiters, the first one to send the winning candidate's résumé to the company's recruiting manager gets the fee. If the company finds the hired candidate, then none of the contingency recruiters receives a fee. Because contingency recruiters are usually in a high-speed candidate chase, they submit résumés to clients as fast as qualified candidates are identified and screened, and they usually do not wait to gather a slate of candidates.

Retained executive search firms are under exclusive agreements with clients to find the best person to fill an open position. With very few exceptions, only one retained firm is paid by a client to present at least five to ten qualified candidates. The exclusivity arrangement between recruiter and client has an important significance to the job seeker. If a company is using a retained recruiter for a particular search, the retained recruiter will submit a slate of candidates, usually five or more, and the recruiter is the only gatekeeper authorized to submit candidates. The only other way to be considered for a position in the client company is to go directly to the hiring company. More importantly, when you are researching competing candidates in subsequent interviews, you will know that the recruiter who interviewed you also screened the other candidates.

Job seekers should ask both types of recruiters if their résumé will be sent to the client, and they should ask for a reason if it will not be sent. The answer may not be forthcoming or one they do not want to hear.

The recruiter assesses how closely the candidate satisfies the position requirements. Closeness of fit (i.e., has the candidate done it before) is usually the most important criterion in the decision to send the job seeker's résumé to the client. There can be mitigating circumstances that might push the recruiter to send a résumé, even if the candidate is not a "perfect" match. If a client search is lengthy and the recruiter divulges to you that very few qualified candidates have been identified, then you may get lucky. Emphasize relevant strengths and attempt to convince the recruiter to send your résumé to the client as a test case to see how flexible the client is regarding closeness of fit. Recruiters sometimes apply this tactic because it may enable them to submit additional candidates if a client reacts favorably to the trial candidate.

Professional appearance and soft skills are other key criteria in the send/not send decision. If the position requires clear, articulate speech for telephone sales calls, a résumé will not be sent if the candidate does not communicate well. If the candidate is interviewing for a consulting position with extensive customer contact, his appearance must be professional and immaculate.

 Make it easy for the recruiter to include your résumé in the group being sent to a client. For each candidate, first-rate recruiters prepare a background summary describing how closely the position requirements are satisfied. If you are fortunate to know the requirements in advance of your recruiter interview, bring a list of the requirements followed by a brief description of your relevant experiences and accomplishments that demonstrate how closely you satisfy each requirement. Depending on the initial dialogue between you and the recruiter, this list could be sent by e-mail before the interview or presented in hard copy form during the interview. If presented during the interview, you should update the summary immediately afterwards based on new information you learned and include it as a WORD document attachment to your email thank you note. Most recruiters would be delighted to receive your summary, which would be edited and sent to the hiring client if you succeeded in convincing the recruiter that you are a viable candidate.

Updating the Recruiter

If you were sent to a company interview by a recruiter, then it is common courtesy to provide the recruiter with feedback after the interview. The one certainty in the search process is that the recruiter will call you if you do not call immediately after an interview. The recruiter will ask you to describe what transpired with each interviewer. Do you think the client liked you? Did you like the interviewer and the company? Who did you meet? What questions were you asked? What is the interviewer's personality? Did the interviewer describe the position requirements the same way I did? Were you told the timeframe for the next step?

A recruiter can be helpful and smooth over a faux pas that occurred during the interview, so it is in your best interest to provide interview feedback to the recruiter. If you forgot to describe an important vignette or to include it in your thank-you note, you can ask the recruiter to mention it. Finally, most company contacts ask recruiters what the candidate thought about the company, and you want the recruiter to be in the position of saying that you were very interested.

There is one risk to be aware of when updating a recruiter on the details of an interview. Candidates submitted by recruiters are your competitors in this high-stakes game and only one of you will win. Although most recruiters are professional and ethical and do not intentionally share information about one candidate with another, slip-ups can and do occur. In their zeal to prepare each candidate for an upcoming interview, recruiters may inform other candidates of a question you were asked or an environment you experienced.

To increase your chances of winning more points than your competitors, you should erect a firewall to prevent other candidates from accessing company intelligence you uncovered during the interview. If values were assigned to information a job seeker can gather in an interview, the highest value would go to the description of position requirements, followed by interviewer personality assessments, company politics, and cultural information. Filter out or play down this and other pertinent information when briefing recruiters and other individuals who might be in a position to accidentally jeopardize your candidacy. Chapter 5 describes how you can obtain this valuable information and achieve a competitive edge.

Hiring Manager

The hiring manager is the person to whom the job seeker will report and the one who will have the most influence in the hire or not-hire decision. This is the person gatekeepers must impress by sending qualified candidate résumés. Other key responsibilities of the hiring manager are to evaluate performance and recommend salary increases, promotions, or termination after candidates are hired. The hiring manager's career is often tied to the success or failure of new employees.

During an interview with a hiring manager, focus on convincing this person that you have performed the position requirements and are excited about doing them again. Do not "brag" about how much more you can do to expand the responsibilities or scope of the position. Too many job seekers blurt out all of their skills, and many are not relevant. If a candidate describes too many skills unrelated to the position, the hiring manager might jump to one of two conclusions: the candidate could become a threat or the candidate is overqualified and will quickly get bored. Concentrate on your ability to satisfy the basic position requirements plus closely related ones.

A unique concern of hiring managers is the question of whether the job seeker has the professionalism and other soft skills to represent his department at company meetings and industry conferences. Hiring managers do this and expect the same of their staff. Introduce vignettes that describe how you successfully represented your department at outside events and inside previous companies by interacting with senior management and peers in other departments. You would win many game points if you are able to cite the trust that your previous supervisor had in you to represent the department and company.

A good question to ask the hiring manager would be What accomplishments would you and your management like to see in the first few months? This question demonstrates your understanding of this person's responsibilities and your response to the reply should

convince interviewers that previous accomplishments resulted in promotions for recent supervisors.

Senior Management

Senior management in most companies are the chairman of the
board, the chief executive officer (CEO), chief operating officer
(COO), and vice presidents. Job seekers who are at the senior management level or just below typically interact with senior management within the scope of their responsibilities, and it is likely that one
or more of the management team will be among the interviewers. A
member of the senior management staff might also interview recent
college graduates, middle managers, and administration staff for selected positions as a matter of company or management policy. Key
requirements of senior management include possessing leadership
skills; demonstrating individual thought with the ability to disagree, albeit in a professional manner; blending in with company culture; representing the company at outside events; thinking strategically; and
being a team player. Be sure to establish a likeness with one or more
of these traits.

Jerry was in the midst of interviewing at an international company
with headquarters based in a major U.S. city. Because 60 percent of
the employees were located in the United States and the remainder
in more than thirty countries, there was a conscious effort by all employees to avoid referring to the company as a U.S. company. Most
employees were multilingual and had previously lived outside the
United States before joining the company. Jerry was multilingual and
had lived and worked in Europe. He successfully interviewed with the
VP-HR, the VP-finance, two directors, and a manager, all from different departments. Jerry and one other finalist were scheduled to
meet with the president, who would have the most influence over the
hiring decision.

During the interview with the president, Jerry was aware of the
strong need to be sensitive to other cultures and to play down the role
of the United States in company operations and decisions. His strategy was to differentiate himself from the other candidate. Although
he assumed the other candidate had similar skills to get this far in the

interview process, he felt it was important to stress his language skills and passion for international travel and foreign cultures.

There was one vignette that Jerry counted on. He seized the opportunity to describe the time he was assigned to live and work in Spain. The first few weeks were spent in a hotel to get acclimated to the environment and to decide on which part of town he wanted to live. He mentioned that he immediately enrolled in advanced Spanish language and history courses. When it came time to decide on where he and his wife should live, there were two choices. The first was to rent an apartment in an American enclave. The other choice was to live in an apartment complex where his would be the only American family. Jerry chose to be immersed in the culture of his Spanish neighbors, and he told the president that this was the best decision he could have ever made. A job offer followed the next day, and Jerry had a most memorable three years with this international company. The VP-HR later told Jerry that this story got him the job offer.

Peers

Most interviews include one or more peers. Imagine yourself in their situation and do everything possible during the interview to put them at ease with your candidacy. Trust is near the top of the list of criteria for a peer interviewer. A supportive and friendly attitude is close behind. Current employees want to go to the office and work on company challenges with someone they enjoy being with, who will support them in a staff meeting, who will assist them when needed, who will speak highly of them to others, and who could become a friend. There is always competition for the boss's attention, but most peers like a work environment without extreme competitiveness. Pick the right vignettes to project the helpful and cooperative side of your personality. Ask how you could help or work with the interviewer if you got the job. Emphasize that you want to do your job well and that you have several references who would say that you have a reputation of helping others succeed. Do not disclose skills outside the scope of the job—you might be trespassing on their turf. Ask what the peers expect and limit your discussion to satisfy those expectations.

Subordinates

A small percentage of companies permit one or more subordinates to interview their potential boss. Be prepared and be sensitive to subordinate feelings. Their worst fear is that you will terminate them shortly after you start your new job. They also worry that you will reorganize the department, change their job responsibilities, or threaten the stability and tranquility of the work environment. One or more of them might also be applying for your job or might have been rejected from consideration. Do not alienate them. One veto and the game is over. You should address these issues indirectly by describing how you handled similar situations and achieved positive outcomes for your previous subordinates.

For example, "At my previous company, I was asked to lead a team of seven whose backgrounds were not known to me. I met with each person to determine their strengths and to obtain their recommendation on how they could best participate in a high priority project. Some minor adjustments in responsibilities were required and resulted in expanding the skills of each team member and implementing the project on time and under budget." Do not make any promises or volunteer ideas about what you would do in the first months of employment. If asked to respond to a question about your plans, respond by describing how you determined the needs at previous companies and developed tailored plans to accomplish company objectives. You would expect to take a similar approach in your next position.

Other Interviewers

The recruiting manager or HR staff will normally inform you of the interview schedule and names and titles of interviewers in advance. In each situation, you should make the interviewer comfortable by stating that you have interacted with the person's functional position in previous jobs. For example, if you are applying for a marketing position and the sales director interviews you, provide some vignettes describing how you achieved great results working as a marketing manager with the sales staff in a team effort. If you are a systems analyst interviewing with a controller, describe how you improved financial systems by working closely with your previous company's controller.

After your first round of interviews, you have done all you can to get a favorable call from the recruiting manager. When the great news comes that you are wanted back for another round, you will have the opportunity to build on relationships made and interviewing skills learned.

Other Game Formats

The most widely used interview format is the one-on-one, face-to-face interview set in an office environment. There are a variety of other formats in which interviews are conducted, and an awareness of the common venues will enable job seekers to remain confident and comfortable with the different situations. The strategies followed by job seekers regardless of the interview format should be the same as the face-to-face interview experienced by Susan, with minor differences in execution. The following are other common interview formats and guidelines on how to succeed with each.

Telephone Interview

There are two types of telephone interview: (1) scheduled in advance by a recruiter or a representative from the hiring company and (2) a surprise call from a recruiter or HR staff member. The purpose of both types from the interviewer's perspective is to determine if the job seeker's experience and qualifications are close enough to the position requirements to warrant an invitation for a personal interview. The most common outcome for interviewers is to screen out unqualified candidates and save many hours of interview time.

The candidate's objective in this conversation is to schedule a person-to-person interview with the recruiter or company executive. This is accomplished by establishing rapport, convincing the caller that you have 'done it before' and want to do it again.

Preparation is critical. An important and obvious fact to realize about a telephone interview is that the interviewer cannot see you. The desk where the expected call will be received should be covered with as much reference material as possible and the tools to go along with that material. You should have the following ready:

✔ Your résumé

✔ A glass of water

✔ Cover letters sent in response to job ads

✔ Computer with high-speed Internet access so that you can open the company's web site and database of contacts

✔ Several typed pages of well-organized vignettes

✔ Notepad and pens

✔ Typed answers to typical interview questions discussed in Chapter 3 and other sources

✔ The general answer to a version of the often-asked, "Tell me about yourself"

✔ List of reminders that includes a broad smile that will be felt at the other end of the phone line, erect posture, confident and strong voice, and the need to approach a likeness with the interviewer

The Scheduled Call

The scheduled telephone interview has the advantage of preparation time afforded the job seeker. Erin's telephone interview demonstrates how well he played the game. He had several days to prepare for a telephone interview with the human resources director of a local company. Everything was going well throughout the call until the HR director asked for his recent salary. Erin's research uncovered the base salary of the previous person in the position, and the HR director was not aware of this major intelligence coup. Erin had a base of $90,000 and the previous person was earning $80,000. He was prepared for this question. Because the company had a great reputation in the industry of Erin's choice, and the functional responsibilities would provide him with a great career opportunity, Erin was willing to accept a lower salary. His reply to the HR director was confident and direct:

> Based on our discussion, it appears that I have per-
> formed many of your position requirements in my last
> job. More importantly, I am very excited about this op-

*portunity, and it could be a win-win situation for both
of us. My base is a little more than $80,000 and salary
is not as important as the people I work with and the
challenges I face in a new position. If you would be willing to meet with me, I can assure you that salary would
not become an issue.*

Erin successfully preempted the salary issue, he achieved his objective by being invited for an interview and he ultimately accepted an
offer of $85,000.

The Surprise Call

A huge prize for every job seeker is a surprise call from a recruiter, a
company recruiting manager, or networking contact with an interest
to explore a job opportunity. Although Murphy's Law states that the
call will come at the most inconvenient time, you should be prepared
as best you can for this important moment. Resources needed to
carry on a productive conversation should be within an arm's reach
of your telephone. There is no second chance. Avoid being flustered
or caught off guard and have material previously listed available at
your fingertips.

Helen received a surprise call from a recruiter one evening at 8:30
P.M. The recruiter introduced himself and the name of his firm. He
immediately reminded Helen that she replied to an e-mail address for
a sales manager ad on an Internet job data bank. Another common
reason for a recruiter call is to describe a search assignment and to
ask if the person has any referrals to possible candidates or other
sources. Helen remembered the ad, which was clearly within her
sphere of experience and interest, and she immediately got into a
selling mode. As in any telephone interview, her objective is to schedule a person-to-person meeting with the interviewer. She tries to accomplish this by convincing the caller that she has performed the requirements before and wants to do it again.

Helen knows she must speak clearly with a confident voice that
projects a professional and competent person. If she has a weak or
hesitant response and is asked by the recruiter more than once to
speak louder, Helen will have a very short conversation and hear the

unpleasant words, "I'll get back to you." After a cordial introduction, Helen asks for the recruiter's contact information and records it for future reference.

At a point Helen believed rapport has been established, she boldly asks for a face-to-face interview to continue the discussion. If she is correct, the recruiter should agree to schedule an interview. Helen is prepared to rearrange her schedule to accommodate a request for an interview. She knows that recruiters fill up their available appointment times very quickly, and if she must call the recruiter back with her availability, there will be no interview.

After the interview is confirmed, it is safe and appropriate to ask a few questions before hanging up the telephone. Helen asked for a copy of the position description, and the recruiter agreed to send it via e-mail. In a very polite way, she also asked the recruiter if he could disclose the name of his client. Unfortunately, this was a confidential search with an incumbent and disclosure was not possible. Many recruiters prefer to wait for a face-to-face meeting before disclosing a client name. If Helen were told the company name, then she would delve into the preparation described in Chapter 1.

In some instances, job specifications are not close to a job seeker's background. In those situations, build on the rapport you established and provide the recruiter with one or more names of associates who might be good sources or potential candidates for the position described. Your purpose at this point is to provide the recruiter with an incentive to call you again to inform you of future searches. One might be for you.

Videoconference Interview

A videoconference system permits someone at one location to see and hear a person or persons at another location. The distance between the connections can be a short walk or a twenty-hour airline flight. Both locations include a PC or TV monitor with a speaker system, a camera, software, a microphone, and a connection to a telecommunications network.

Large and small companies and executive recruiters alike are increasing the use of videoconference technology to conduct interviews with job seekers located in other cities. These companies are using their own in-house systems or reserving videoconference facilities offered by industry vendors and retailers. A video connection is less costly and more time efficient than paying for airfare, hotel, and hosting a job seeker for an interview.

Some job seekers may be intimidated and uncomfortable with this technology. Knowledge of what is to come will increase confidence and prospects for a successful interview. Before your first or next videoconference, visit one of the vendors offering the service and ask for a briefing on the capability and preparation required to use it. According to Chuck Duvall, a specialist in videoconference systems, the following are some helpful suggestions.

What to Wear

➤ Do not wear brilliant colors such as reds, yellows, or greens. These colors will cause "flaring" on the receiving end.

➤ Do not wear plaid or broad pin-stripped shirts, blouses, sweaters, suits, or jackets. These patterns might appear as color bars at the receiving end.

➤ Dress conservatively and use solid, neutral colors.

Arrive Early to Set Up

➤ Get familiar with the room setup and practice using the controls for sound volume, camera placement, and zooming capability.

➤ If possible, try to arrange the camera so that your background is a wall with a solid blue or gray color, which are especially effective and friendly in appearance.

➤ Do not sit in front of a window or bright light. Backlighting will make you appear dark and feature-less. Close drapes or blinds.

➤ Position the camera in such a manner that it will not see any movements through doors or windows. These will be distracting for interviewers.

➤ Depending on the videoconferencing system, the camera should be located on top of the monitor for that "personal" interactive look that permits good eye contact.

➤ The camera should be directed at the upper body so that you will not distract the interviewer with objects on the table or if you take notes.

➤ Vignettes, résumé, and any reminder notes should be strategically located on the table in front of you and out of camera view. As preparation, type this material in large font and in outline format so that it can be read without much head movement. Minimize downward glances to read.

➤ Ask for advice on placement of the microphone. Some video-conferencing systems have an audio echo.

➤ Most videoconferencing systems use what is called a "boundary microphone." These microphones are usually directional and should be placed on a hard surface like a table or desk. The microphone should be oriented toward you and usually not more than 24 inches away.

➤ The microphone should be positioned in such a manner that it will pick up your voice but minimize the noise created by shuffling of papers or the sound of a computer fan.

➤ Be sure to obtain the telephone number to call if assistance is needed and an interviewer's cell phone and video number at the interviewer's location.

Getting Started

➤ Turn off cell phones, pagers, and telephone ringers during the interview. Any ringing will be embarrassing.

➤ Develop a mind-set that the interviewer is located across the table and inside the camera, which should be directly above the monitor.

➤ Sit upright, relaxed, and do not slouch.

➤ The first impression is just as important on video as it is in person. Ensure a broad smile, confident, clear, strong voice, and direct eye contact with the camera. Everything except the handshake.

➤ After introductions, each party should ask the other if they are able to see and hear clearly. Make any necessary sound or camera adjustments if asked to do so and request same if needed.

➤ If there is more than one person conducting the interview, write their names in the order in which the interviewers appear on screen.

➤ Most of the newer videoconferencing units display motion close to actual speed. Some systems will appear to be in slow motion. You should keep movement to a minimum, with an occasional slow moving hand gesture and the frequent smile. Avoid arm waving or fast movements.

➤ Some systems have a sound delay from the time you see an interviewer's mouth moving until you hear the words, as in newscasts from around the world. Make sure to wait until the interviewer finishes their sentence before you respond.

➤ Do not rock in your chair or enter into a nervous state of perpetual motion. Take a few deep breaths to avoid that occurrence.

➤ If an overhead presentation is used, the minimum character size should be 14 points. Background and character colors should be contrasting so they can be seen on the remote monitor clearly. Make sure to test your presentation for readability before using it for the first time.

➤ Minor glitches in audio and video will occasionally occur during the interview, and they should be overlooked and ignored. The conversation should be carried on as normally as possible, without any distraction. Your focus is the same as an in-person interview—convince the interviewer that you have performed the position requirements and are excited about doing them again. Be sure to convey passion and energy.

> Avoid the tendency to be lulled into a bored state with no one in the room.

> Do not be distracted by background sights behind the interviewers. Focus on the camera.

A Meal Interview

One of the most embarrassing things than can happen during an interview is to spill a cup of coffee on the interviewer's desk or splash soup on your tie. Accidents do happen, but there are precautions that job seekers can take when having a meal interview. Place a napkin on your lap, keep elbows off the table, and do not use your fingers to eat. Read about proper use of utensils and take a lesson on table manners. Grabbing a fork to attack your food can surely result in having your last meal with that company. If you are applying for an international position and your interviewer is using chopsticks or utensils in a manner unlike an American, then you may do the same if you are comfortable doing so. Eating style takes practice to master in any culture, so do not attempt a new approach for the first time during an interview. Take small bites so that the interviewer does not have to wait too long for you to clear your mouth, be decisive when ordering, leave your napkin on the chair when standing up, and avoid poor manners like soaking gravy onto a piece of bread.

Meal interviews tend to be more social than other settings and there is usually a blend of unrelated topics mixed in with serious interview probes. Do not fall into the trap of relaxing or bearing your soul. Your objective remains the same as in any first interview, so stay focused. If there is more than one interviewer at dinner, then also follow the guidelines for a panel interview. Do not bring a notepad to this interview. Rather, have a small pad and pen readily available in your jacket pocket or purse. Position requirements should be jotted down if there are too many to remember. Note taking is very distracting to all parties during a meal, so be very selective about what notes you take.

Paul responded to an ad for a management consultant position at a prestigious firm. He has expertise in building infrastructure in developing countries and the firm is looking for someone to head up that consulting practice. Paul was called immediately by one of the consultants after reviewing his résumé, and a lunch interview was scheduled. The consultant conducting the interview had been assisting the senior partner in the firm with the interview process for the previous four months. Paul was focused on playing the appropriate vignettes and exhibiting interest and energy throughout lunch. As they were both finishing their entrées, the consultant startled Paul. He told Paul that he was the best candidate that had been interviewed in four months, and he was going to recommend that he meet with the senior partner. Paul was excited and went a bit out of character by telling the consultant, "It can't get any better than this! I am really excited about the opportunity and am looking forward to meeting the senior partner. Would you mind if we skipped dessert?" The interviewer laughed and asked for the check. If the interviewer says that you will be invited for a second interview, then your new objective becomes to end the interview as quickly as possible.

The following are additional guidelines for a meal interview:

➣ Do not order an alcoholic beverage, even if you are the only person drinking soda. Most interviewers will understand that you want to have a clear and sharp mind for the interview.

➣ Wait until the host picks up the menu before you look at yours.

➣ If you have a weight problem, you should be conscious of ordering healthy foods. An overweight person who eats a fattening meal with French fries and tops it off with a whipped cream dessert will not leave a favorable impression.

➣ Order food that is easy to chew and can be managed with a fork or easily balanced on one. Cherry tomatoes have been known to fly four feet across a table when not pierced at the correct angle. Be sure to cut them with a knife first. Salads and omelets are safe meals.

➣ Do not order food that must be picked up with your hand, like spareribs, or something that can splash or drip on your tie like soup. Some sandwiches are fine as long as the contents will not squirt at you or the interviewer.

➤ Order something with a moderate price and avoid choosing one of the most expensive items. Lobster is a very poor choice; besides, it is difficult to eat.

➤ Ask the host for an entrée recommendation or follow the lead of another person at the table.

➤ Do not be the only person to order dessert. If the interviewer orders dessert, you should also order dessert; otherwise, order coffee or tea so that you will have something to drink while your host is enjoying dessert.

A Panel Interview

An interview with four people at the same time can be intimidating and overwhelming. View this interview as a discussion with four people, one at a time. That means four handshakes and four first impressions. You should be given the names, titles, and contact information of each panelist in advance of the interview. Do your homework and find out as much as possible about each person before the interview. Plan to arrive at the company location fifteen minutes early. If you are lucky, you will be led into an interview chamber and asked to wait until the panel members arrive. They will likely enter the room at different intervals just prior to the prescribed start time.

Take advantage of the few minutes you might have alone with each panelist as they enter the room. Introduce yourself and focus on your first impression. In the few minutes you might have, obtain a business card, and attempt to find out something personal about the interviewer or if there is a previous connection. This is your chance to bond and establish a friendly face among the interrogators.

When everyone takes a seat to signal the start of the interview, arrange the business cards facing each person. The leader of the panel will ensure introductions have been made and set the ground rules and tone for the interview. Be sure to maintain direct eye contact with each questioner as you begin your response and slowly move your eye contact to each person as you complete your answer. Referring to each panelist by name at least once during the interview can be impressive.

Informational Interviews

Job seekers initiate these interviews with individuals who hold positions in a functional area or industry they wish to learn about for possible employment. What better way to find out about the intricacies of a particular job than to speak with someone currently doing it? These meetings may also double as practice interviews for those looking for a first job or with limited interview experience. Recent graduates uncertain about a career direction should conduct informational interviews to explore the many options available. Other job seekers may initiate these interviews for similar reasons, to pursue a long-standing passion, or because the industry in which they have worked for many years has negative growth and no jobs.

Interview Objectives

The primary objective of these interviews is to learn what it is like to work in a particular job function or industry. When contacting someone to schedule an informational interview, state that you will only require twenty or thirty minutes and that you will be sure to end the meeting on time. State that the purpose is to obtain information about a particular job function or industry. Do not mention that you want to discuss getting a job—that could prevent the meeting or stop information flow during a meeting.

Unlike the job interview on which this book is focused, job seekers during informational interviews should be encouraged to ask questions similar to those they might ask when evaluating a job offer. The following are some of the many questions job seekers may ask to enable them to learn and to make an evaluation regarding level of interest:

➤ What are some unpleasant aspects of the job?

➤ What skills are required?

➤ Where can the career path lead in a few years?

➤ What are industry publications or information sources?

➤ Can you recommend any courses, training sessions, conferences, or seminars to expand my knowledge?

➤ Are many companies profitable or experiencing financial difficulties?

➤ Where are some places to look for jobs in your industry?

➤ Can you suggest another person for me to meet with to have a similar informational meeting?

➤ Do you have any advice?

Where to Find Contacts

Start with the familiar and expand outward in imaginary concentric circles. Tap into your innermost circles of family, close friends, neighbors, community acquaintances, business associates, and so on. Then move into your virtual networks of university alumni, employees from previous companies worked, and members of industry/professional associations.

   Those entering the workforce upon graduating from high school or college might understandably have a very small circle of contacts. If you are in this situation, gather ten to twenty of your friends in a similar situation and organize and lead a networking meeting. The purpose of the gathering would be to help each other identify informational interview prospects. Pair up the attendees and ask each person to describe the background of individuals being sought. The goal is for each person to leave the meeting with an informational interview prospect.

Every Meeting Is an Interview

The reason informational interviews are discussed in this book is because every informational interview can become a potential job interview. Informational interviews are often gateways to the underground or hidden job market, which is a major source of newly created or unfilled jobs. Individuals with whom informational interviews are scheduled may know about jobs in their company or at other companies in the industry. For that reason, job seekers should treat all informational interviews as a screening for a potential job interview. Unbeknownst to you, the person you meet might be aware of a job opportunity, and he is sizing you up to see if you have the required qualities and could be referred without being an embarrassment.

Be vigilant for possible job opportunities at all times, even during a seemingly low-pressure informational interview. Although the meeting was scheduled because you wanted to find out about working in a particular field, it would be wonderfully fortuitous if an actual job opportunity for you to explore was described.

Preparation

Before an informational interview, you should conduct much of the research described in Chapter 1. Demonstrating knowledge of the company and person with whom you are meeting would be an excellent move. The more you impress, appear likeable, and offer help, the more in return you should receive. An important and special element of preparation for informational interviews is determining in advance how you could possibly help the person you meet either personally or professionally. Perhaps you could refer the person to a friend who might be a potential customer. At the very least, the end of the meeting should include a personal thank-you for time spent and a sincere request that the person call you if there is anything you could do to reciprocate.

You are now prepared for your second and subsequent interviews.

Chapter 5

Differentiate Yourself: Second and Subsequent Interviews

Interviewing is not a gentle sport. The game reaches a crescendo going into the second round of interviews as you now compete with a small number of candidates, perhaps less than five. Each competitor must be eliminated before you can win the interview game. Interviewers will dispose of a few, but you must help them to remove the rest.

This chapter describes aggressive tactics to differentiate you and to build on the great perception created in the first interview. Candidates who reach second and subsequent rounds normally satisfy basic requirements for the position, and those who differentiate themselves in as many ways as possible will remain standing at the end of the day. Remaining focused, impressing interviewers in subsequent interviews, gathering competitive intelligence, and applying powerful differentiation techniques are presented in this chapter.

Focus

Many job seekers who get this far develop the false impression of being in the homestretch and they let their guard down. Some of these candidates established a great rapport with company managers and begin to "loosen up" and share weaknesses that they successfully avoided sharing in the early interviews. That is a fatal trap set by experienced interviewers. Keep in mind that there are only a few candidates being interviewed at this stage of the process, and all of you generally satisfy the position requirements. It is only a matter of degree based largely on soft skills and a weak compliance with a particular requirement that separates one candidate from another. You are still selling—do not be lulled into a state of true confessions.

Do not do due diligence. The urge to ask questions that will help you to decide if this is the company you want to work for must be suppressed, as it should have been in the early interviews. Due diligence should be performed in silence, outside of earshot from any company manager. Remain focused in selling mode with an upbeat, positive attitude, and an obvious interest in the company and the position. Winners in this fierce competition do not ask what the company can do for them; rather, they focus exclusively on what the company needs and how they can help to accomplish those needs.

A Second Interview

An invitation to a second round of interviews may involve meeting with some of the same people from the first interview plus a lineup of others you will meet for the first time. It is becoming more common for interviewers, particularly hiring managers, to meet more than once with selected candidates. The purpose is to obtain as much assurance as possible that the person is qualified, has the right personality to be successful, and gets along well with everyone.

Although your second and subsequent interviews will likely be arranged and coordinated by someone in the human resources department, you will normally not be interviewed by the HR contact more than once, unless an offer is in your future. You will also not meet with a recruiter more than once, but you should update the recruiter after each interview. The remaining interviews will be with the hiring manager and others designated by the hiring manager and HR professional. Although most interviews will be with company employees, there will be instances when the company's auditors or an independent consultant retained by the company will be asked to assess your skills. Interviewers usually complete an evaluation form for each candidate. The form generally includes an assessment of strengths, weaknesses, personal qualities, and how closely position requirements are satisfied.

Second Interview, First Interview

You did well in the first interview and are invited for another visit to the company facility. Consider the perspective of those with whom you will be meeting for the first time. One of the gatekeepers or the hiring manager informed these new interviewers that you passed the initial screening interview. New interviewers are told that there are some aspects of your background that the company requires, and their objective is to confirm your strengths in those areas. As with all interviews, part of your evaluation will be to determine if you can "fit" into the organization personally and professionally.

All may not be perfect. There might be one or more skills that the hiring manager was not certain had the depth of experience the job requires and asked new interviewers to explore further. It is also possible that a new interviewer does not like the idea of hiring another person in her department and she is looking for reasons to reject your candidacy.

The approach taken by Susan should be used as a primer for each first-time interview, including preparation, first impression, response to the, "Tell me about yourself" request, vignettes, thank-you note, and everything described in the preceding chapters. You are still in sell mode. There is one additional perception you could create, if appropriate. If you previously met with the hiring manager, even in the past hour, identify all positive points mentioned about your background and all the points you made that were positively received by the hiring manager. There are some interviewers, especially subordinates, who might be influenced by the opinion of hiring managers.

If you believe that the hiring manager's opinion might influence a particular interviewer, casually inform the interviewer of one or more positive comments that the hiring manager shared with you. Do not use this tactic with more than one person, because it might backfire if interviewers realize that you used the same approach more than once. For example, suppose the hiring manager's name is Darren and he responded favorably in your interview last week when you replied to his request to describe your experience managing engineering projects from concept formulation to production, which is one of the position requirements. You should tell the subordinate interviewer what Darren said, "Darren asked the same question and he told me that my previous role at Success Engineering Company was exactly as he requires here. Let me describe my previous role. . . ."

Some interviewers like to know their supervisor's opinion before they form their own.

Second Interview, Second Interview

Preparation for a second and subsequent interview with someone met in the first round is essential and requires creativity about what should be emphasized the second time around. The documented results of the first interview are critical when preparing for the second interview. If you had a good first meeting with an upcoming interviewer and were successful in identifying that person's view of the position requirements, then you should prepare additional vignettes that demonstrate your proven ability to perform those requirements. You may use one or two vignettes mentioned in the first interview to serve as a reminder, but be sure to include new ones to reinforce your candidacy. If weeks have passed between interviews, you should confirm that the position requirements have not changed. Do this by asking and listening.

Consensus Opinion

Not only do hiring managers want to meet candidates more than once, they want to obtain a consensus opinion from supervisors and peers. This helps to ensure an objective assessment and to share the blame if the candidate is not successful. The need for a consensus opinion can generate frustration for all parties involved. The managing director at an investment banking firm asked several contingency recruiting firms to find a financial analyst. The résumé of one candidate impressed the managing director and she wanted to be the first to interview the candidate. Her administrative assistant scheduled the interview with the managing director and one of the managers in the human resources department. The morning after the interview, the administrative assistant called the recruiter with feedback indicating that the managing director believed that his candidate was a winner. That was the good news. The bad news was that there were nine user department managers that the new person would be interfacing with, and the managing director required that the candidate meet with each one as part of the interview process.

Almost two months had passed by the time the exhausted candidate met with the ninth line manager. The managing director informed the recruiter and the candidate that a written job offer would be sent to the candidate within two business days. During the previous two months, the candidate continued to interview elsewhere and was fortunate to receive a written offer from another company. When the promised written offer from the investment banking firm was replaced by two questionable excuses, the candidate decided to accept the other offer. The candidate was disappointed, the recruiter lost a sizable fee, and the managing director had to start the interview process all over again. The managing director has since been fired.

Competitive Intelligence

Top tennis players know the strengths and weaknesses of their competitors. One has a great backhand, another is recovering from an ankle injury and will weaken fast in a running game, yet another has a great net shot or a weak second serve. A winning tennis strategy is to attack an opponent's weaknesses and avoid playing to their strengths. Preparation for second and subsequent interviews should follow the same strategy. Learn the strengths, weaknesses, and personalities of competing job seekers and then use that competitive intelligence to strengthen your candidacy during your next interview.

The competitive clichés of no pain, no gain or no risk, no reward apply in a huge way to the highly competitive interview process. Complacent job seekers do not win. Smug athletes going into a final round of their sport as the favorite often lose when they focus too much on avoiding mistakes rather than taking risks to be the best. The second, third, or fourth placed athletes who risk life and limb are the ones who can surpass the top players because they have less to lose and everything to gain. Sarah Hughes, competing in the women's figure skating event at the 2002 Olympics in Salt Lake City, is an excellent example of this phenomenon. She was fourth going into the final round of skating and she knew something spectacular must be done to impress the judges. She completed the most difficult routines in a perfect performance and won the gold medal over world-class performers who were too cautious to attempt the high-risk routines. Job seekers must consider the risks and rewards when obtaining and applying competitive intelligence.

Information Sources

Recruiters, company interviewers, and networking contacts are your sources for information about competing candidates. During your first round of interviews with any of these sources, interviewers will be attempting to reduce a large number of candidates down to a manageable few who will be invited for second and subsequent rounds. Your pursuit of competitor backgrounds in this first round should not be proactive because most will be eliminated from the process; rather, you should only listen for clues about other candidates. These clues might take the form of a passing remark: "We are only sending the client résumés of candidates who have recently held the title of Sales Manager for at least 5 years," or "Only industry experts will be recommended to our client," or "Only those with more than $50 million of profit and loss management will be considered," or "We are only considering candidates who have recent Fortune 500 experience." Listen for the following information about competing candidates—it can be extremely helpful in second and subsequent interviews:

> What do hiring company executives like about other candidates?

> What skills are most candidates lacking?

> What are unusual qualifications or attributes of other candidates?

> Why was someone eliminated from consideration?

Recruiters

The first place to go for information is the recruiter who sent you to her client. A retained recruiter will have interviewed every competing candidate, while a contingency recruiter might have interviewed only one or two of the total candidates being considered by the company. Recruiters call their candidates to schedule company interviews and provide the itinerary. Many recruiters prepare candidates for an upcoming interview. At the end of this preparation discussion, you should thank the recruiter and ask what company executives like about the other candidates. Wait for a response. If the recruiter tries to be helpful but does not know, then ask a follow-up question about a desired quality other candidates do not possess or inquire about what company interviewers said about any of the other candidates. If a retained recruiter refuses to respond to your questions, then there is no recourse and move elsewhere.

If a contingency recruiter presented you to the company, ask him if you are the only candidate he has in the interview process. If you are, then the contingency recruiter is also competing with candidates from other recruiters and should be cooperative when asked about other candidates. If he has no knowledge of other candidates, then you should suggest that the recruiter ask his company contact for information. If the contingent recruiter has more than one candidate being interviewed, you should still ask for information about the other candidates as previously described. You should do so in a casual manner and not make a big issue about the request. Do not disclose to the recruiter how you plan to use this information. Be vague about the reason and state that it will be helpful when you are interviewed in the next round.

Company Interviewers

It is always best to obtain a strength or weakness of another candidate without asking, but these instances do not occur often. An inquiry about other candidates requires a good rapport with the interviewer, and care should be taken to avoid appearing too aggressive, too meek, or too desperate with the inquiry. You should be confident and a bit inquisitive when asking about other candidates. This questioning should be pursued with only one interviewer because it would be viewed negatively if two interviewers discover that both were asked about other candidates. Be certain that the person you select has interviewed other candidates and knows the comparison you seek. The human resources contact or the hiring manager would be excellent targets for such a discussion, but other less experienced interviewers might be more receptive to your request. One way the inquiry can be made during a second or subsequent interview is to ask,

"Based on your interviews with other candidates, what strong qualities have you identified?" A follow-up question is too risky because it could create the impression that you are more concerned about other candidates and less about the job.

Networking Surfaces Another Candidate

Through personal contacts, your goal should be to identify someone who knows another candidate interviewing for the same position. An introduction to that person would be an excellent outcome.

To reach a networking target, you must divulge the name of the company where there is a job opening. This presents the risk of new candidates inserting themselves into the interview process without you knowing it. The secret is to control the list of people with whom you share your request for information. Use your networking skills and express your needs with personal and professional contacts you can trust and with members of networking groups you know well. Identifying one of these types of networking sources can provide invaluable information for you to use in your next interview.

The best aspect about networking is that the results can be unexpected and helpful at the same time. Imagine in the course of networking that a friend told you that her friend, Jill, is interviewing for the same job at the same company! You can ask your friend how well she knows Jill and to get your friend's opinion about how much Jill can be trusted. If you get a good feeling about your friend's relationship with Jill and the extent of trust you can place in her, ask for an introduction. If you know that there is at least a third candidate, then inform Jill that your purpose in calling is to ensure that you or she will win that important job and not one of the other candidates. Three candidates means each of you has about a 33 percent chance of winning, but if you eliminate one candidate, the odds for the remaining two candidates increases to 50 percent.

If the two of you were the only finalists, then your purpose for calling Jill would be to keep each other informed of interview progress. One of the most frustrating aspects of interviewing is waiting for feedback. Another candidate to commiserate and share information with can make this unpleasant period more tolerable. Good net-

working skills can identify other candidates more than most job seekers think. The two candidates brought together by networking may take the following approach to strengthen their positions:
Get to know each other.

➤ Do not inform the recruiter or the human resources contact that you know each other.

➤ Share the results of previous interviews, including interviewer personality, views on the position requirements, company timing for a decision; strengths, weaknesses, or comments made about other candidates; information about reporting relationships; and any other helpful information.

During subsequent interviews discuss with each other how to emphasize strengths that you both possess and that you know other candidates do not have. If you and your new "buddy" stress the importance of a particular skill, then you might create a perception in the minds of interviewers that other candidates should have that skill.

After subsequent interviews coordinate follow-up calls to the recruiter or human resources contact. Call one of these gatekeepers to obtain updates and insights on the interview process. Determine which questions would provide the most useful answers and assign the questions to each other to ensure that you do not ask the same ones. Suggestions for questions include those that relate to timing of final decisions, number of other candidates remaining and their strengths and weaknesses, the hiring manager's availability (is she going on vacation soon?), salary levels, company views on relocating a candidate, or any number of factors about what is going on.

The search experience of Boris and Chuck provides an example of how candidates working together can lead to up-to-date information, less frustration, and a positive attitude. Both belong to a large networking group and the members know each other well enough to have established a good level of trust. At one of the meetings, Boris asked the group for information about the company where he was interviewing for a management position, and Chuck exclaimed that he was interviewing for the same position. They met immediately after the meeting and agreed to share everything and to help each other. By that time, Boris had interviewed with the recruiter and the hiring manager, and Chuck had interviewed with the recruiter and the VP-HR. The last interview for both was two weeks earlier.

A few days after they agreed to help each other, Chuck got a call from the recruiter, "Chuck, the company wants you to know that they really liked you, but two candidates who more closely satisfy the requirements are being interviewed. Keep in touch. We both know the situation can change at any time." Although Chuck was disappointed, he asked the recruiter about the two candidates being interviewed to see if he could obtain some helpful intelligence for his friend. The recruiter did not provide any information. Chuck immediately called Boris to inform him of the latest developments. Boris expressed disappointment for Chuck and told him that he was just called by the recruiter and is scheduled to meet with the VP-HR. Since Chuck had interviewed with the VP-HR, Boris benefited from all the insight Chuck could offer.

Three weeks elapsed since Boris interviewed with the VP-HR and several voice and e-mail messages to the recruiter remained unanswered. Boris was upset and frustrated to the point where his search efforts slowed to a crawl. He had to find out where he stood in the process. It was obvious the recruiter was ignoring him, so he asked Chuck to call the recruiter to find out what was going on. Because the recruiter had already told Chuck that he was not being considered, his call was not a difficult one for the recruiter to answer. The recruiter informed Chuck that there were two finalists. The one recommended by a Board member was given an offer this week and the company was waiting for an acceptance. Boris got his answer and moved on with his search, perhaps weeks before the recruiter would have told him.

In another situation, Rita and Cameron responded to the same healthcare administrator ad and they agreed to keep the other informed of their responses. Rita was the lucky one who got an invite for an interview and Cameron was told that other candidates more closely meeting the requirements were being interviewed. Rita proceeded through the interview process and was given an offer. Fortunately for Rita, she had two offers and chose to accept the other more lucrative one. Rita had the difficult task of informing the company that she would not accept their offer.

Before meeting with the hiring manager, she remembered that Cameron was also interested in the position. She called Cameron and found out he was still looking for a job, and Rita told him that she was going to recommend him to the hiring manager. She met with the hiring manager and described her reasons for accepting the other offer. She then told the hiring manager that she had the perfect candidate for the healthcare administrator position and recommended very strongly that the hiring manager meet with Cameron. Such a recommendation normally is very credible because Rita was very professional and had gotten to know the company culture and management team well enough to receive an offer. The thought of starting the search process over again was daunting to the hiring manager, so he called Cameron. Cameron was interviewed, given an offer, and still remains with the company. That is the ultimate reward of networking.

Stacking the Slate

Networking can take a strange twist during the interview process. If you see the benefit of sharing information with another candidate as previously described, then there is a way to derive the same benefit by planting a candidate and carrying out the same "buddy" scenario. The risk is that you might introduce the hiring company to the winning candidate and you would finish a distant second. Recruiters provide clients with qualified candidates to be considered for a position. There is a maximum number of candidates that recruiters will forward to clients and that number differs from client to client and search to search. Their goal is to have a winner and two runners-up in the slate. If there is no recruiter and you are interviewed directly by company management, then there is a minimum number of candidates that must be interviewed to provide management with the confidence that they have fully explored available talent in the marketplace before extending an offer.

If in your interview with an executive recruiter or a company recruiting manager you become informed, and convinced, that the search is just beginning and a slate of candidates is being formulated, then you may wish to consider this approach. Within your networking circles, look for another job seeker who might also be qualified for the position. Describe the search and inform the person of the recruiter or company contact. Make certain you obtain a commitment from this person to be totally open and honest and to share with you every aspect of their interview experiences. You will be doing this person a huge favor by identifying a new job opportunity, so the best choice would be a good friend you trust and with whom you get along well. Keep in mind the benefits and risks and consider the possibility that the other person might win the job offer. The major benefit will be to have two "insiders" on the same team as competitors in a small group of candidates. Work this opportunity well and one of you has a high probability of winning the interview game.

Networking Identifies Key Contacts

Networking has the potential to identify sources that could provide job seekers with competitive intelligence and a competitive advantage over other candidates in the midst of the interview process. Two valuable sources are a company interviewer and an employee, current or former. Being referred to someone who knows an interviewer or company employee can result in catapulting your candidacy to the top. Approach this advantage in a professional way or you may be viewed as too aggressive and shatter your chances for an offer.

Suppose a friend knows the hiring manager or the VP-HR. The best possible scenario would be if your friend knew either of these contacts well enough to meet the person and to sell them on your credentials. A less intrusive way your friend could help you would be to write a brief note to the key company player. The note could describe how well your friend knows you and how capable you have demonstrated yourself to be in previous job situations. You might even suggest some of the contents of the letter to make it relevant to the position requirements.

A third approach is for you to inform the hiring manager or VP-HR that your friend can be used as a reference and to suggest that the friend be called to provide another opinion about your candidacy.

This request could be made during a subsequent interview, in a thank-you note, or while you are waiting for feedback.

A similar scenario could be followed if a networking contact knows a current or former employee at the company. Do not be concerned with the level of the employee to whom you are referred. The most important factor is how well the employee knows the hiring manager or VP-HR. If you are comfortable with your contact's relationship, then you should consider calling the employee. Your options for obtaining the employee's help are similar to finding a friend of the hiring manager or VP-HR. Meet with the employee and discuss if and how the person might be able to help your candidacy. One suggestion would be for the person to write a note to the hiring manager or VP-HR stating, "My friend whom I have enormous respect for introduced me to Bob Thompson today. I understand that Bob is interviewing for the Lead Engineer position. My friend recommends him very highly and I wanted to pass that information along for your consideration. In my meeting with Bob, I can substantiate my friend's opinion." The note can continue by stating that your friend will also serve as a reference.

How to Use Competitive Intelligence

The use of information about other candidates must not be perceived as a personal attack against any individual. If you uncover a competitor's strength, attempt to achieve parity by demonstrating a comparable strength without disclosing knowledge of another candidate's background. If you identify another's weakness, describe how that weakness is a particular strength of yours. Let interviewers assume the desired conclusion.

Terry was interviewing for a director of sales position in a small company and was scheduled to meet with the vice president of marketing and his potential boss, the vice president of sales. In the final stage of the interview with the vice president of sales, Terry expressed his high level of interest in the position and asked if there were any areas that he could expand upon to ensure that he gets an invite for another interview. The vice president of sales liked Terry and wanted to be honest with him. Terry was informed that there was only one other candidate being considered and that the other candidate had a larger rolodex than Terry but was not as good a closer when it came to sales presentations. In another interview, the vice president of marketing mentioned how important closing skills were for the new director of sales. A few days after this interview, Terry was informed that there would be one more interview before a decision is made. The final interview is to be with the chief executive officer (CEO).

Terry was lucky to obtain information about another candidate from company interviewers without asking for it. Careful use of this information when he met with the CEO got Terry a job offer. Early in the interview Terry asked what the CEO's top need was. It was a great setup question because Terry knew the answer. This was a sales position and the answer provided by the CEO was immediate revenue. Terry then commented that any person taking this position must have proven closing skills to be successful, knowing that was the other candidate's weakness. Terry continued with controlled excitement by describing vignettes of how his closing skills previously resulted in immediate revenue generation. To make this strength come to life, he mentioned that references will be able to attest to his closing abilities.

In addition, Terry complemented his important closing skill with the fact that he also had a rolodex to keep him busy generating new clients. He continued to describe how he would apply his networking, cold-calling, and other sourcing skills to attract more clients. A final point Terry made with the CEO was that he would be able to hit the ground running, taking just a few days to learn about the company, its product lines, and current and target clients. It was possible that the other candidate had a large company mind-set and would recommend weeks or a month to plan. Terry emphasized that he would plan and prospect for clients at the same time—that is the small company approach.

The use of background information about a competing candidate can be applied in many ways. The objective should be to emphasize your strengths relative to the position requirements, and at the same time, highlight the competitor's weaknesses. Suppose you are interviewing for a position at an Italian company with international office locations, and you know that the competing candidate has international experience but little exposure to Italian culture. You should describe vignettes that demonstrate you are in many respects more like a company employee than your competitor. Convince the interviewer of your understanding of Italian culture, history, political issues, geography, travel, food and so on. That would be a winning move. The following are examples of relevant skills and experiences you should mention, if you have them, to put you on a pedestal above other candidates.

➤ Worked for an Italian subsidiary with reporting relationships to the corporate parent in Italy. Built consensus, understand employee/management protocols, and know how to get things done.

➤ Worked closely with an Italian vendor or client.

➤ Lived in or traveled extensively throughout Italy.

➤ Conversant in Italian or studied the language in high school or college.

➤ Conversant in languages where international offices are located.

➤ Spent time on a student exchange program with a family in Italy.

➤ Recognized as a connoisseur of Italian wines.

Differentiation Techniques

Competitive intelligence on competing candidates combined with differentiation is a powerful combination that leads to job offers. A positive emphasis on your unique qualifications as they relate to the position requirements can result in your candidacy rising above the competition. The time taken to identify areas in which you can differentiate yourself will be time well spent. Many job seekers have successfully applied the techniques described in the following paragraphs. The possibilities for inclusion on this list are limited only by your creativity and imagination.

The application of differentiation techniques should be a closely guarded secret from the recruiter, networking contacts, and any individual involved with your search. This extraordinary need for secrecy may appear to be a touch of paranoia, but if other candidates use the same tactic there would be no differentiation.

Leave Behind

The only item most job seekers leave behind after an interview is the résumé. This presents an opportunity to stand out from the rest of the pack and to demonstrate your writing skills, analytic ability, and other differentiating qualities not easily conveyed in an interview. Cole was interviewing for a Director-Mergers & Acquisitions (M&A) position. During most of the interview, Cole was asked to describe the M&A transactions in which he played a significant role. At the end of the interview, he provided the hiring manager with an impressive two-page list of M&A transactions in which he had a lead role.

Extreme care must be taken to avoid grammatical and spelling errors, otherwise, your document will become the equivalent of a "pink slip." Other examples include a web developer who left behind a long list of web sites she developed, an advertising account manager left behind samples that he completed for a major publication, a financial manager gave his prospective boss a complex Excel spreadsheet, and a marketing manager left behind a business plan. Each of these examples demonstrated past accomplishments that could convince an interviewer you can do the same thing again for their company.

The previous examples were historical documents used successfully by job seekers. Giving an interviewer a description of a future plan has significantly greater risk to your candidacy because of its subjectivity. Brad interviewed for a senior management position, and, based on his advanced preparation, he developed an action plan that he would follow in the first sixty days of employment. About halfway through the interview with his prospective boss, he was fairly confident that his plan had a likelihood of success. He presented the unsolicited plan and Brad's high-risk approach paid off. The manager liked it and an offer was subsequently received. The outcome could have gone the other way just as easily, but Brad knew there were other candidates being given serious consideration and he felt that he had to take a risk.

A document need not be presented during the interview. If the interviewer emphasizes the importance of developing a business plan or other document that you have prepared in a previous position, then include the document as an attachment to the thank-you note and you have executed a winning move.

Solve a Problem

An interviewer may divulge a pressing company problem during an interview. If you encountered a similar problem at a previous company, your description of how you solved the problem could get you to the next step in the interview process. As an alternative, you could offer to enter into a consulting arrangement to demonstrate the value you could bring to the company. If company management were impressed with your interim work, there could be a full-time job offer upon completion.

Richard was interviewing for a sales position and was told that the company had a problem expanding into a new industry to sell its products. Halfway through the interview, Richard was asked to describe the extent of his rolodex in the desired industry. Without a moment of hesitation, he removed from his attaché case two stacks of business cards. He told the interviewer they were all less than two years old and his call would be accepted by every person. The interviewer thumbed through the cards and immediately arranged for Richard to be moved through the interview process at which time he received an offer.

Humor

Stiff, nervous, and boring describe the stereotyped image of an inexperienced job seeker. Humor could be just what the doctor ordered to isolate you from the competition. This does not mean you should share your favorite joke, even if you are asked to do so. The risks of offending an interviewer or appearing foolish are too great. You should also not attempt to create laughter more than once in a one-hour interview or you may be viewed as a jokester. However, demonstrating that you have a sense of humor could win you a job offer.

Jack was interviewing for a graphic designer position and was scheduled to have a final interview with his supervisor. Jack's research uncovered a lot of information about the interviewer, her likes, dislikes, and personality, which included a good sense of humor. The interview was going along well for the first twenty-five minutes as the supervisor spoke continuously about the company, the employees, and expectations for the position. At that point the supervisor realized that Jack did not have an opportunity to say anything and she remarked, "Jack, you must think I am full of hot air with all the information I am throwing at you." Without skipping a beat Jack replied, "Well, it has been quite warm in here for the last half hour!" The supervisor burst into laughter and told Jack he had all the qualities needed for the position. The next day Jack received an offer and accepted it.

Provide a Preliminary Reference

An acquaintance with a high profile or a senior executive known to company management where you are interviewing can be used as an effective differentiator. For example, if you know that the hiring manager is on the board of the local United Way, and you happen to have a close relationship with one of the board members, this technique should work well. Obtain permission from your board member acquaintance before your upcoming interview. At an appropriate time during the interview, you might say I spoke to Emily Parson on the United Way board about meeting with you, and she insisted that you call her to obtain another opinion about me. If the interviewer does not call Emily within the next few days, you may ask Emily to take the initiative and call the interviewer. Before asking Emily to make that call, be certain that the call would not be viewed as too intrusive or too aggressive.

Pete had an interview scheduled for the next week. During his preparation, Pete observed that he and a manufacturing manager at the hiring company previously worked at the same company but did not know each other. Two members of that previous company's management team were Pete's references, and he used a winning technique in his interview. As the interview was closing with the hiring manager, Pete mentioned that he was aware that the company's manufacturing manager, and he previously worked at the same company and that the person likely knew two of his references. Pete provided the names of the two references and suggested that the hiring manager ask the manufacturing manager to call them. This would ensure an objective reference and provide the hiring manager with confidence that he was getting honest feedback.

Emphasize a Strength

Different weight is placed on each position requirement. If your most significant strength happens to be the top priority position requirement, then that is your most important asset to emphasize during an interview. Most candidates will have a range of experience in some or most of the position requirements. You should present well-thought-out vignettes to make it impossible for other candidates to be as strong as you in the most important requirements.

Personal Connection

Except in rare situations, company executives prefer candidates with prior personal or professional knowledge of their industry, company, management, or products. Following are two examples of job offers that were the result of personal connections.

A job seeker, Caroline, responded to an ad for an administrative position at a nonprofit organization that coordinated the exchange of high school students among host families around the world. In her response to a job ad sent to the human resources director, Caroline said that she had a personal experience with the organization. That piqued the curiosity of the HR director enough to schedule an interview. The first question asked in the interview was to describe the personal experience with the organization. Three years earlier when Caroline's daughter was in high school, she applied for an exchange program under the auspices of this organization. Caroline subsequently received an offer and experienced three exciting years with the organization as a result of a personal connection.

In another example, a systems analyst was interviewing for a position with a manufacturer of audio equipment used with PCs and high-quality sound systems. During the interview, the candidate described his hobby of recording music for local bands. When he mentioned that his recording studio was filled with the company's products, the interviewer's level of friendliness and acceptance changed immediately. The candidate received and accepted an offer directly as a result of the musical connection.

Location, Location, Location

Human resources executives know that Murphy's Law has a high incidence of occurrence to jeopardize a relocation situation. The winning candidate's spouse, children, in-laws, or some friend or relative will likely identify, or create, a reason for not completing the relocation within the time frame stipulated in the offer letter. Although HR executives who have a relocation budget want to fill key positions with the best and most qualified candidates, regardless of where they currently reside, there is always serious and preferable consideration given to qualified candidates who live within commuting distance of the company facility.

If you are a local candidate in a search where one or more competing candidates must be relocated, you are in a tremendously advantageous situation. Make certain the hiring manager and the VP-HR are aware that you have an easy commute to the office. A gentle reminder should be mentioned, such as, "I reviewed a web travel site and it recorded the distance and time from my home to this location incorrectly. My drive this morning only took 30 minutes, not the 50 minutes quoted."

The location issue can take on relative forms if all candidates are local. A short drive from the company office can be an advantage over candidates who live more than an hour's drive away. A vignette that works well if you have a short commute is to describe how a company emergency required that all key employees get to the office as soon as possible. Cite how several employees were dependent on a train schedule, others required an hour's drive, and you walked ten minutes to the office. That can be a powerful argument for your candidacy.

Entrepreneur Versus Large Company

Executives at small, entrepreneurial organizations usually express skepticism when they come across a job seeker who recently left a $1 billion company after twenty years. Candidates with a large company background interviewing at small companies must create the perception of being successful in a small company culture.

If you have adequate small company experience, you had better flaunt it to ensure favorable consideration for a position with a small company, for example, "After I left a Billion Dollar Company three years ago, I joined a young technology firm as its fourth employee. The company grew to 150 employees and was just sold. That is why I am seeking another opportunity." This story convinced the hiring manager that the job seeker made a very successful transition from a large to a small company. If you know that one or more competing candidates are currently working for large companies and have not yet made the transition, then you might play to your strength and their weakness by saying to the hiring manager, "It takes a special person to make the transition from a large to a small company. During my first three months, I never thought I would adjust to the entrepreneurial environment. It was the patience and tutelage of my boss that enabled me to have a successful transition. I am certain you cannot afford to have someone like my previous boss to help new hires adjust."

Small companies generally have smaller budgets, less staff, and shorter deadlines than large companies. These are critical but often unwritten requirements for all new employees. Describe vignettes that demonstrate your experience with these needed skills and you will have played the game well.

Visit Company Sites

When interviewing with a bank, retail chain, or company with multiple offices, take time to visit a few branches, stores/locations. Observe employees, procedures, cleanliness, products, and make a purchase or conduct a transaction if possible. Look for good examples of courteous employees, user-friendly procedures, product features, or services not available at competitors. Find some advantage over the competition. Observe why products are purchased or not purchased, listen to questions customers ask, and obtain a first-hand observation of the sales process. You should also ask the store/branch/purchasing manager for some observations about the product.

During the interview, mention that you visited a branch or local store and were very impressed, especially with the product line that is not available at competitors, or some other positive observation. Candidates in transition should have ample time to accomplish these visits and that will be an excellent differentiator from employed competitors who are too busy commuting to the office. Your visit to company locations with an objective, positive assessment demonstrates a high degree of interest, energy, and initiative—all excellent qualities few competitors will have.

Be Audacious

There are instances when a hiring manager is arrogant, blunt without regard to personal feelings, domineering, or has a strong-willed personality. Fortunately, individuals with these unpleasant qualities are not encountered often, but it is important to know how to react to such behavior when it occurs. This is an opportunity to stand apart from competitors who might be intimidated by such actions.

If you are like most people, these qualities are not what you would like to face on a daily basis. However, if the job responsibilities are terrific, other employees are easy to work with, and you are able to extract sufficient respect from the hiring manager, you might overlook some negative personality traits. An approach that works with this difficult personality is again the concept of likeness—act in a similar manner but to a lesser degree. The operative word is "act" because you will be required to go outside your comfort zone, but the payoff can be worth it.

A job seeker interviewing for an HR position learned in advance that the hiring manager possessed some of the qualities previously mentioned. The interview was brief, less than ten minutes. The hiring manager began by saying that his boss forced him to hire someone for the position and that it will have the least authority among his managers. The candidate was not intimidated and injected some humor. He knew the hiring manager had teenage children as he did, and he replied that the authority he will have appears to be the same as he experiences when reprimanding his teenagers. The second and final question posed by the boss was in a very arrogant tone. The hiring manager held up the candidate's résumé and berated the candidate by saying, "This résumé does not convince me that you know anything about human resources and why should I hire you?" The candidate's reply was expressed with a touch of resentment and in a very firm, confident voice while pointing to the same résumé with a stabbing finger. He said, "You're right, that résumé doesn't show one tenth of what I can do for this company! I handled tough employee relations situations, recruited management teams, and instituted excellent benefits—all critical needs you have right now. That's why you should hire me." He got the offer.

Plant a Reference

Recognized protocol for reference checking is to ask the candidate permission before contacting a reference. This guideline is not always adhered to. Some human resources professionals and hiring managers attempt to identify common acquaintances having a past connection with candidates. It should be no surprise that those mutual connections are often called without obtaining your permission. While that smacks of being unfair, job seekers can play the same game.

As part of interview preparation, uncover the background of company management, members of the board of directors, outside consultants, and all interviewers. Determine if any of these individuals previously worked at one of the companies you did, live in your hometown, belong to the same volunteer organizations, have children the same age as yours, or have some connection to your professional or personal life. Assuming that you have a positive relationship with one or more of these common connections, you may prepare one or two as a reference and ask them to act surprised if called by a company representative. Playing a common connection can be a winning move in the interview game.

This can be accomplished during the course of an interview by the old name-dropping technique. Do this with only one name and be sure not to include this person in your list of references provided to the hiring company. For example, in the course of conversation, you should casually say something like the following:

> I worked closely with Tina Buxley, the financial services industry expert, on a few projects.

> Tom Surley, the CEO of Cyber Sales Company, and I worked together on an important joint venture.

> I was on a panel last month with Ted McLearner, the head of Human Resources at People Consulting.

The bait has been set. If you are a serious contender, and the names you mentioned are known by one of the interviewers with whom you set this trap, they will likely be conducting what they think is a clandestine reference check. They might even attempt to use networking contacts to be introduced to the person you mentioned.

Unique Combination of Skills

Skills that only you and a very small number of people might possess can set you apart from other candidates. Companies are recognizing secondary skills that support or complement primary skills required for the position. Secondary skills can differentiate you from competitors. The following table provides a small number of the many possible examples of unique combinations of skills that should be stressed during an interview.

Primary	Secondary
Finance	Technology Skills
Marketing	Finance Skills
HR	Sales Skills
Information Technology	Marketing Skills
Manufacturing Operations	Human Resource Skills

Leadership

Leadership is a skill that applies to almost any position, and it manifests itself in different ways. If this quality is missing from a position requirement description, there is a strong likelihood that it is an unwritten requirement that will be viewed very favorably. At the project manager through senior officer level, vignettes should demonstrate leadership by describing examples where you conveyed a vision for growth; achieved teamwork, employee loyalty, budgeting controls; and abided by the leadership principle of MBWA (management by walking around). Describe your project management roles for multiple projects that achieved objectives both within budget and time frames. Cite instances where you set the example for your team. Candidates do not demonstrate this trait often and your examples will go a long way to help your candidacy.

If your marketing plan calls for the staff to speak at industry conferences, describe when you were the first to do so. If you asked your team to work on a weekend to meet an important deadline, be proud to cite when you joined your team on a sunny summer Saturday and helped to proofread, copy, and perform other tasks necessary to get everyone home as soon as possible. Taking the initiative is another rare quality and applies at every level. Describe when you performed tasks that were not within your area of responsibility in the interest of helping other teams and completing company projects on time.

Multitasking

Regardless of the position for which you are interviewing, a winning differentiator can be to demonstrate the ability to perform several complex tasks at the same time. Conveying this skill with appropriate vignettes should project the perception of being intelligent, well organized, focused, and competent.

Volunteer for the Unwanted

There are jobs that have unpleasant requirements and many candidates cannot or will not perform those tasks. This presents yet another opportunity to stand out from competing candidates. For example, a job that requires extensive travel may not be desired or wanted by someone with a young family. Take advantage of the fact that interviewers are not legally permitted to ask candidates about their personal lives. Volunteer pertinent information to convince interviewers of your ability to travel and to work long hours when necessary. Indicate that you have no family restrictions and accumulated enough frequent flyer miles for two trips around the world, presuming it is true. This demonstrates you are sincere and able to undertake such a strenuous responsibility.

Working a night shift either full time or as needed is another potentially difficult work requirement that should be handled in the same manner as travel. If there is a choice between a day shift and night shift, offer to work the night shift if you can. Very few candidates would do that and you should have a competitive edge. After six months or a year of excellent performance, you should be able to apply for a day job if you wish by coming through the back door as an employee.

Personal Values

Most job seekers correctly describe functional skills and experiences as portable assets for use in a new organization. Be among the few who identify personal values. Resourceful, self-motivated, ethical, honest, results-oriented, and community volunteer are a few values worth mentioning during an interview. Do not list them as a matter of fact. Use passion, exhibit confidence, and come across as being proud of your values. Avoid mentioning religious or political affiliations in these discussions.

International Experience

If you have any international experience, flaunt it. Many companies have offices or customers abroad and an equal number of companies aspire to that situation. Extensive international travel, living in a foreign country, and ability to converse in more than one language can be a great asset at many companies. The company being interviewed may have, or plan to have, offices where your language ability could be in demand or the company may be trying to sell their products and services to an ethnic group who speak your second language. Previous experience living or working abroad could also win you a job offer with your first-hand cultural experience. If you have any contacts in a country where the interviewing company is seeking to do business, be sure to drop that fact casually during an interview.

Short Learning Curve

All new employees have a learning curve before productivity can be achieved. Demonstrate knowledge of company products, competitors, customers, employee names, and convince interviewers that you know more than the average employee. By the time candidates reach second and subsequent interviews, this knowledge becomes one of the differentiating factors in selecting a winning candidate.

Announce Another Offer

The mere mention to a hiring manager or a human resources officer that you just received a written offer from another company creates the perception that you must be good at what you do if you played the interview game elsewhere and won. This disclosure should be made at the end of an interview, after rapport has been established, and immediately be accompanied with the proclamation that the company with which you are interviewing is clearly your top choice. Also state that the reason you are divulging the existence of an offer is to request that the interview process be accelerated and come to closure before you must reply to the other firm. Juggling one offer against another is a hard ball tactic discussed in Chapter 6. The biggest risk to job seekers is that the hiring company might say there is no intention of rushing the process and good luck with your offer. Think through possible ramifications before taking this move.

Another use of this disclosure is to create a quantum leap in credibility regarding your experience and capabilities. For example, Gerardo was interviewing for a supervisory position managing one-hundred employees. During the interview with his potential hiring manager, Gerardo was told that the company is concerned about his management capabilities because thirty was the most employees previously managed. At that point, Gerardo informed the interviewer that he just received a verbal offer (that was the truth) for a position managing three-hundred employees. Supervisory skills were no longer an issue to the interviewer because of the other offer. The same positive effect might also be achieved by stating that you are currently interviewing for positions with responsibility for many more than thirty employees.

Formatted Résumés

Many of the major recruiting firms rewrite candidate résumés to ensure they all look alike and appear bland to their client. These recruiters do not want clients to be impressed with résumé format. The problem that Jan uncovered at one company interview was that the recruiting firm presented its client with a résumé that had a typo for the dates worked at a particular company. Fortunately, that error was subsequently corrected, or Jan's job offer could have been jeopardized. Job seeker recourse when submitted by a recruiter to a client company is to provide a formatted résumé to the human resources interviewer to compensate for possible typing errors and to demonstrate your formatting skills. Take every opportunity to look better than competing candidates.

Conscientious

An important quality sought by employers and often measured in personality tests is conscientiousness. Do not say that you are conscientious, rather, lead the interviewer to that conclusion by citing vignettes where you produced a complete and accurate report, went the extra mile to deliver a project on time and within budget, or received compliments from your supervisor for how meticulous you were to ensure a quality outcome.

Stress Situations

Some professions require zero tolerance for exhibiting symptoms of stress, emotion or empathy. These jobs usually involve responsibility for the lives of others, such as airline pilots, air traffic controllers, nuclear engineers, research scientists with volatile products and similar high stress positions. When interviewing for one of these jobs, take the initiative to describe vignettes that demonstrate your coolness and logical action in crisis situations. You should convince interviewers how serious and capable you are regarding critical safety and security issues surrounding the position for which you are applying.

Job seekers also have an opportunity to differentiate themselves when interviewing for jobs at the other end of the stress spectrum with a high volume of customer interaction. Many of these jobs require employees to listen to clients, be empathetic to their needs, and build rapport early in the conversation. Those who excel in this type of job usually must leave their emotions behind when they recommend to the customer a sound business or professional solution. Demonstrating with vignettes your ability to understand client needs and provide sound, logical solutions will differentiate you from competing candidates. Examples of these jobs include customer service and call center representatives, career counselors, consultants, psychologists, and sales positions.

Other Examples

The following examples could also differentiate you from other job seekers. Don't hesitate to mention appropriate examples if they are not apparent on the résumé.

- ✔ Few job changes in recent years
- ✔ MBA from any school, especially a top one
- ✔ Bachelor's degree in the field required by the position requirement
- ✔ Good listener
- ✔ Accomplished musician
- ✔ On the board of a local charity
- ✔ Leadership role in an industry association
- ✔ Adjunct professor in a local university
- ✔ Unusual hobby
- ✔ Personal relationship with a recognized person

Susan's Second Interview

Susan was interviewed by only one person in her first interview—Scott Gilbert, the VP-HR. Two weeks later she received a welcomed call from Scott's administrative assistant Amanda. Susan was asked if she was available the following Tuesday for a second round of interviews, and she confirmed her availability without hesitation. Amanda informed her that upon arrival she should ask for Scott who would introduce her to the first interviewer. She was scheduled to meet with her immediate supervisor (the VP-marketing), a marketing manager (her peer), a subordinate, and a person from another department with whom she would have considerable interaction.

Everyone but Scott was a first-time interviewer and Susan immediately began her preparation. She reviewed the extensive material gathered before her first meeting with Scott, the detailed notes taken after the interview, and she called networking contacts to uncover information about the new interviewers and other candidates. Susan knew that she must repeat her interview performance with Scott for each new person and determine appropriate differentiating factors to play.

Tuesday arrived and Susan smoothly moved through each interview. She chose to differentiate herself by demonstrating in-depth knowledge of both the publishing industry and membership-driven businesses. An unexpected connection was discovered when Susan and the marketing manager realized that they had a mutual industry acquaintance. Susan called that person immediately after leaving the company premises to inform the acquaintance that she might be called as a reference.

Susan sent thank-you notes to each interviewer and waited for the next phone call.

PART III

WINNING MOVE: ENJOY THE MOMENT

6 | Negotiate Final Hurdles:
The End Game

In the previous few months, you met with a seemingly endless list of interviewers in three visits to company headquarters. Almost three weeks to the day from your last interview you receive a voice message from the human resources contact. It could have been from a recruiter if there was one. As you return the call, you prepare for the worst and hope for the best. The human resources contact immediately puts you at ease by saying, "We would like to check your references." Be excited but do not spend your first paycheck yet.

There are a number of significant events that must take place from the moment you receive such a welcome call to your first day on the new job. You are asked to provide the names, professional relationships, years known, and contact information of three references. If you were asked to provide references in an earlier interview, you are now told that these people will be contacted. In addition to reference checks, offers at some companies are subject to satisfactory background investigations and a personality test.

The objective of Chapter 6 is to give you the information to close the deal. You are provided with a winning approach to selecting and preparing references, receiving an offer, performing due diligence (this is your choice), authorizing a background check, and taking a personality test. Fortunately, you have some degree of control over all of these tasks.

Reference Checking

Every employer checks candidate references. It is the prudent thing to do. References are always verified for the top candidate and some employers call references for the top two or three candidates. When references are checked for several candidates, responses become another measure for comparing finalists and selecting a winner.

How many job seekers provide references with whom they had bad experiences? Company representatives also know the answer. There are some human resources professionals and executive recruiters who are excellent at conducting reference calls. They ask very specific questions that permit little or no wiggle room, and they can sense a negative opinion from a hesitation or an attempt to avoid answering a question. If you are lucky, one of these capable interviewers will not conduct your reference checks.

Who to Select

At some point early in your search you should identify five to ten references. Companies usually ask for three or five, but you should have additional references to avoid using the same ones too often and to have the choice of picking the best reference for each company. Reference selection is a reflection on your candidacy. Selection criteria should include references with whom you have an excellent rapport, a trusting relationship and who agreed to provide positive and supportive comments. Each person should be able to vouch for your excellent work relating to several of the position requirements.

There is a perception among employers that the more senior the reference, the more credible the assessment. Play on that perception when selecting references. Regardless of your job level, seek out the most senior person at the companies you worked at most recently to serve as references. If you were a programmer and completed a major project recognized by the chief information officer (CIO), ask the CIO to be a reference to discuss your performance on that project. If you were a market research analyst and the vice president of marketing is aware of at least one of your major accomplishments, add that person to your list. If you were a vice president, ask the president or a board member of your recent company to be your reference.

Immediate supervisors are always requested and providing two would be impressive. Sales and business development candidates could include one or two customers who can vouch for your professionalism, proposal presentation, and closing skills. Another credible reference is an outside consultant who can substantiate your technical expertise. The most powerful references are individuals recognized in their industry, public figures, or senior management at a recognized company. When candidates provide high-profile references, prospective employers might have a brief conversation or sometimes do not call because they assume comments will be highly supportive.

The best time to ask someone to be your reference is shortly before or after your departure from your recent company when you are remembered and the sympathy factor is still strong. If your reference would like to write a letter praising your abilities, accept the letter graciously but indicate that many companies prefer to make a personal call. When asking a person to be a reference, indicate that you will use their name as few times as possible and will contact them in advance of a call. It is a nice touch to send a brief e-mail to each reference every month or two during the search to keep them informed of your progress.

Preparing a Reference

Recruiters and human resources professionals call references to verify employment history and to determine previous performance. Your references may be from a few jobs ago and may not have seen or spoken to you in a number of years. To ensure that they will be outstanding references, you should obtain permission each time you need it. When a reference agrees to accept a call, describe the opportunity and key areas the person should emphasize. Mention that you will send an e-mail with pertinent information. Good references will carry the following list to ensure it is available when called:

➢ Name, title, and phone number of person likely to call

➢ Company you are interviewing with

➢ Job title and brief description of position for which you are interviewing

➢ A reminder about your connection to the reference: company worked, position held, your responsibilities, and dates worked

➢ Accomplishments that the reference would know about to bolster perceived weaknesses and highlight desired strengths

➢ Soft skills that you would like the reference to convey

Exhibit 6-1 is an example of an e-mail to prepare a reference.

EXHIBIT 6-1 An E-mail to Prepare a Reference

Thanks so much for being a reference. Bill Smith, VP-Marketing, at The Hiring Company will call you this week. The position title is human resources manager with HR generalist responsibilities. The immediate need is to recruit key players in different countries and to create an organizational culture of sharing, cooperating and being team oriented. I would appreciate it if you emphasized the following tasks I performed under your direction.

- I led the recruiting effort for you which resulted in hiring 8-10 senior managers. My specific role was to source candidates, interview all candidates, and arrange for others to interview candidates. The new-hires were all exceptional people who exceeded their performance expectations.

- I started a quality function, trained a key person in your group and obtained support for a function that was generally viewed as not necessary. My excellent interpersonal skills and ability to deal with different personalities made me successful.

- I defined specific goals and objectives related to customer and employee satisfaction and achieved each one, resulting in the organization receiving its largest bonus. Some specific accomplishments were to conduct an employee survey to determine morale and other issues, review HR functions, marketing operations and other procedures.

- You can also mention that I have the very highest ethical standards and professionalism, am very dependable and just a pleasure to work with

Thanks, again. Please call me as soon as you speak with Bill. I hope we can get together soon.

Follow-Up After a Reference Call

Debriefing a reference is critical. Ask references to call you immediately after their conversation to describe the important points discussed. The discussion points are usually the hidden and most critical needs for the position, and you should stress your skills related to the newly surfaced needs in subsequent discussions with company executives. A call to a reference is good news and lets you know that the company is still very much interested in your candidacy.

If an offer is lost at this late stage, try to determine the reason. It might be a reference who faltered during intense questioning. A bad reference is like a double agent who must be eliminated from your list for future opportunities. These renegade references could be the cause of long searches. One way to find out about a disloyal reference is during your debriefing call. You might observe some discrepancies between what you are told by the reference and what the hiring manager tells you. You can also call the HR contact or recruiter making the calls to see if the results are satisfactory and try to discern any remarks that differ from what you were told by your references. A more drastic step would be to seek assistance from a firm that specializes in checking references (perform Google search for "reference checking"). These firms will assign a specialist to call a suspected reference and pretend to be a recruiter requesting an opinion on your performance. You may also ask a recruiter friend to make the same call instead of hiring a firm.

Receiving an Offer

It is still not time to relax! Although a verbal offer allows the job seeker to begin switching from seller to buyer mode, this transition should be made slowly. Do not become a statistic and lose an offer when you are so close to winning the game.

As you move through the land mines of negotiating an offer, your ultimate goal is to transform the terms to be acceptable to you. Successful negotiating strategy includes projecting yourself into the minds of hiring managers and human resources professionals for each negotiating point. Ensure that your desired outcome makes company management feel like winners, they remain convinced you are the best candidate, and they are not offended by your negotiating tactics. From your perspective, let flexibility be your guide throughout negotiation with the objective of closing the deal.

Before hiring executives extend an offer, they want to obtain some assurances that the offer is within range of the winning candidate's expectations and to be sure that the candidate is excited about the company and will likely accept the offer. Hiring executives do not want to go through the motions of an offer with a seemingly uninterested candidate. The recruiter, human resources recruiting manager, or the hiring manager normally calls to discuss an offer with a candidate to assess level of interest before extending a formal offer. You worked long and hard to receive this call. Be excited but also treat the offer as pending until it is seen in written form.

The overture of an offer requires job seekers to perform a delicate dance. The first reaction should always be to express excitement and interest in the opportunity. At the same time, care must be taken not to bite the hand that fed you by reciting your compensation demands. The verbal offer could easily be retracted. You may ask for clarification regarding title, estimated bonus potential, or extent of travel, but do not get into negotiation mode or due diligence yet. The objective of this long-awaited call should be to request an offer letter and sufficient time to evaluate the terms. If you are fortunate, you may have the opportunity to compare it to other offers.

An offer may not be what it seems until all components appear on company stationery. The letter should eliminate any misinterpretation from a phone conversation and may also introduce areas requiring clarification. Do not use the word "contract" when requesting an offer letter—it frightens corporate hiring executives. "Letter" is gentler and is not perceived to have legal overtones. Although CEOs and other senior management candidates normally get contracts to sign, they should also ask for a letter of understanding/agreement containing the significant offer terms before a contract is prepared. The HR officer usually can write the offer letter quickly without an attorney. If the terms in the letter are satisfactory to the candidate, the legal contract can be prepared.

The risk of starting a new job without an offer letter is very high. Tom received offers from two companies. He accepted the vice president of manufacturing offer for a subsidiary of a Fortune 500 company. He obtained verbal offers from the VP-HR and from the CEO to whom Tom would report. The offer was to be presented in a complicated contract that included base, bonus, stock options, severance, and other terms. Standard policy was for the corporate parent to prepare all contracts. Tom requested a letter of agreement, but was told that a contract could be prepared almost as quickly. Because Tom was able to start immediately, he decided to get to work and wait a week for the contract. A week went by and corporate legal sent excuses for the delay. Two weeks went by, a third week, and a fourth. During the fourth week, Tom called the CEO of the company whose offer he rejected four weeks earlier and asked if he could be reconsidered for the position, which was still vacant. The CEO told Tom that he had the same experience in his career. He personally prepared an offer letter that same day and sent it overnight to Tom. The next day, Tom resigned from the Fortune 500 subsidiary and started work three days later at the other company. He was paid as a consultant for the time worked. Tom was lucky, very lucky.

Negotiating an Offer

Although seeds of your compensation desires should be planted early in the interview process, negotiating begins in earnest the moment you have an offer letter in hand. While some cultures expect job seekers to be aggressive negotiators, corporate America is just the opposite. Hiring managers find negotiating an anathema, so if you are satisfied with the terms, avoid uncomfortable discussions with your new boss, accept the offer graciously, and start your new job.

If there is a recruiter, it is usually to the job seeker's advantage to have her negotiate the offer with company management. Recruiters generally have extensive negotiation experience and they remove the candidate's risk of conducting an acrimonious negotiation directly with a new boss. Some negotiations can end in an offer being rescinded or long-lasting negative feelings. For example, a recruiter could shield the candidate from a prospective employer by implying that she, not the candidate, originated any strong demands. For example, the recruiter might inform company management I don't believe that Amy will be happy with $90,000. She would require a sign-on bonus of $10,000 before accepting the offer. Are you in a position to offer such a bonus? A candidate saying this to her soon-to-be boss might convey a very greedy, demanding personality that did not surface during the interview. To a lesser degree, human resources professionals can also be a buffer between candidates and hiring managers.

Ted's example demonstrates the benefit of using a recruiter to close a deal. He received an offer for $160,000, which was $10,000 below what he wanted. The recruiter knew that Ted would not accept the proposed offer and the company would not go a penny above that amount. The recruiter was successful in negotiating a compromise by obtaining a salary and performance review after three months where the base salary would be increased if Ted met predetermined objectives during that period. Ted saw his target $170,000 was only three months away and he accepted the offer.

Do not underestimate your bargaining power when you receive an offer. You may attempt to redefine the terms to your satisfaction, within reason, without appearing greedy, demanding, or arrogant. Successful negotiations can be achieved by being professional, explaining your reasons for each request, and understanding the reasons for the company's position.

If your conditions have not been met to your satisfaction, consider these backup requests if appropriate: (1) a performance and salary review after three or six months, (2) a sign-on bonus when you join, (3) a guaranteed minimum annual bonus regardless of how you or the company perform, and (4) a severance package if you are terminated.

For many job seekers, the most important factor is the base salary. Before forming an opinion about an offer, find out if it is in an acceptable range based on title, responsibilities, geographic location, and other factors. One service that may provide valuable information for negotiating is *www.salary.com*. Other sources for salary data might be industry, professional, or trade associations, and there are also web resources for determining cost of living in relocation situations.

Juggling Offers

Imagine being out of work for twelve months when you find yourself in the final stages of four interviews. Dom had spent most of his career as a controller for technology companies and was searching for another controller position. The first offer was from an out-of-town technology company and would require relocation. Although there was a recruiter involved, his future boss the chief financial officer (CFO) extended the offer personally in a telephone call followed by a signed fax to Dom. It was a nice touch and demonstrated the CFO's desire to hire him. The call set up the protocol for Dom to negotiate directly with the CFO. Dom said all the right things. He expressed excitement about the offer and asked for a few days to reply. Dom wanted this negotiation to take a few weeks to allow the other three companies to formulate offers. The offer terms were generally acceptable to Dom, and he was convinced that he could come to a deal with minimal negotiations.

Dom had two pressing tasks. First he wanted advice from three trusted business associates, his personal "board of directors." His "board" identified the following points for Dom to discuss with the CFO:

1. The offer included a relocation package but did not specify the details of the package.
    Question: Ask for a fixed amount, rather than an allowance for individual costs associated with relocation.

2. The offer did not include a severance package that should be included, especially when relocation is required.
    Question: Ask for a year of severance if the company has a change of control (i.e., new ownership) or if he were terminated. Dom was prepared to accept three months.

3. The offer included financial and administrative responsibility over most corporate functions but did not specify hire and fire authority.
    Question: Ask for authority to hire and fire as needed.

The next day, Dom called the CFO, discussed these three points, and asked for a revised offer. The CFO was receptive to Dom's requests and said that the company's board of directors needed to authorize the changes before another offer letter could be prepared and that might require a week.

The second task was to notify the other three companies and apply the right amount of pressure to get them to accelerate their decision-making process and to extend offers. Before making these calls, Dom had to decide if the first offer were the only one, would he accept it. If not, then he should reject it and wait for the other three situations. It would be like playing Russian roulette to use a job that you would not accept as an excuse to pressure other companies—they will likely tell you to take the other offer. If the first offer is acceptable, then some pressure should be applied to the other three companies to hasten the process, recognizing the risk of losing each one.

Dom decided that he would accept the first offer if none of the other offers were better. On the afternoon of the offer, Dom called the two recruiters and one human resources contact for the other three situations. He informed each that he had an offer and would like to come to closure within seven days because that was the timeline of the first offer. A call of this nature is a nightmare for recruiters and human resource professionals if the companies were interested in Dom and there was no backup candidate. Two days passed and the calls to Dom came trickling in. The second technology company replied that there were a few other candidates yet to interview and they could not conclude interviewing in a week. Dom asked to remain in consideration in the event the first offer fell through. The third technology company had a strong backup candidate and decided to pursue that person rather than be pressured. The fourth company was a local financial services company, which said they would send Dom a written offer the next day.

Juggling more than one offer may be exciting, but it is also stressful and difficult. Timing is the most important factor, and it is rare to have a couple of offers to evaluate at the same time. Within the week, Dom received the two written offers. The first offer for the out-of-town company included a fixed amount for the relocation expense, a six-month severance package, and the hire/fire authority. This was just about what Dom requested. For the first time in a year, he was in control and he was the buyer. What a great feeling.

Comparing two offers is a problem all job seekers should have. The following chart highlights the two offers.

Factors	Local Company	Out-of-Town Company
Compensation	Comparable	Comparable
Location	No Relocation	Relocation Package
Title	Controller	Controller and Administration
Responsibility	Less Than Other Offer	More Than Other Offer
Industry culture	Financial Services	Technology (a Strength)

Dom ultimately decided to accept the out-of-town offer. The overriding reason was that he knew the technology industry and enjoyed working with the major players for twenty years. He did not feel comfortable with the culture of the financial services industry, he had a steep learning curve, and he needed to obtain credibility to perform his job well. The technology industry position would be a better career move with increased responsibility, he would continue to maintain his industry contacts and credibility, and he would remain on a career path to a more senior position when, not if, he changes jobs again. All are good reasons for the decision. The one drawback is that he must relocate. After about five months into his search, Dom agreed that relocation would likely be required and obtained the support of his family in this important decision. Dom received an excellent relocation package that will enable him to make a smooth move. He was very relieved when he told the financial services company that he could not accept the position. He even recommended two excellent candidates and maintained a good relationship.

Rejecting an Offer

Rejecting an offer is more difficult than accepting one. The extent of consideration given to rejecting an offer should be based on the point in the job search at which the offer is received. There are three periods of time that correlate to the level of demand in the marketplace by recruiters and company hiring executives. The first period is when the job seeker is employed. During this time, the job seeker is usually in great demand by competing companies, recruiters, and other employers. Individuals currently employed are generally more aware of job opportunities than their unemployed counterparts because recruiters often call employed contacts as sources for searches. Rejecting an offer during this period has virtually no risk because the current job serves as a safety net. Although there might be a lost opportunity, the job seeker can remain with the status quo and continue looking for that perfect job.

The second period occurs in the first few months of transition from a previous job. Demand for job seekers is still high early in a search and an interesting phenomenon occurs during this period. One or two job opportunities are often identified and lead to interviews and possibly an offer. Many of these early offers are rejected for the wrong reasons. Job seekers falsely assume that if they got an offer so early in their search, they will get other opportunities just as quickly. Demand in the job market diminishes over time and opportunities become less frequent. Rejecting an offer in the first months of a search is fraught with the risk of not finding another opportunity for quite some time.

The third period is many months into a job search. Job seekers continue to be in demand, but at a rapidly diminishing rate. Job offers received during this period should be given even more consideration than those received during the second period. Perform an evaluation by discussing the planned rejection with your personal "board of directors," family members, other job seekers, and associates currently employed. Arrive at your conclusion after weighing the pros and cons. You should be more flexible with regard to salary, title, and responsibilities, particularly in times of relatively high unemployment.

Before informing the recruiter or the hiring executive of your decision to reject an offer, ask yourself the following two questions:

➤ *If I turn this offer down and am still unemployed in six months, will I be angry with myself?* This is not the time to be idealistic or to stand on principles. If there are a few aspects of the job that you do not like, it is possible that the situation can change after you have been on the job for a short time. It is also possible that you can initiate and recommend the desired change once you become an employee. Ideal or perfect jobs are rarely found or they may take years to find. If you believe there is something to learn or the job will benefit you in some way, consider accepting it and conducting an ongoing search from a position of strength as an employed person.

➤ *What components of the offer or aspects of the company situation would have to be changed to make you happy enough to accept the offer?* If you absolutely refuse to accept the offer as it stands, then you have nothing to lose by requesting the changes you require as a negotiating point. Prepare your list of totally unacceptable terms and your desired alternatives. Call the recruiter or company contact and describe the terms that would be satisfactory to you and enable you to accept the offer. For example, if the one-way commute to the office is almost two hours and you do not wish to do that on a daily basis, request permission to work at home two days a week. Nothing ventured, nothing gained. You will also feel better after making this request, regardless of the outcome.

Picking a Start Date

The overriding goal after receiving an offer is to start your new job as soon as possible. Murphy's Law will find a way to rescind your offer during the twilight period between the time you receive one and the planned start date. An endless list of disastrous possibilities could affect your new company or boss-to-be and all hiring could become frozen leaving you in the cold. Health or personal problems could affect your start date. Most of these possible situations would not have affected your employment status if you were at your desk hard at work. An early start date could make you the solution to your company's or boss's problem or you would be able to take sick leave or personal time off for your own problem.

Starting a new job as soon as possible has obvious and hidden advantages. The day you start a new job, some company benefits begin to accrue while others become effective immediately. These benefits include health and dental insurance coverage, life insurance, vacation, 401-K matching and vesting, and the most important benefit of all—the paycheck.

In one situation, Leslie, an environmental project manager, received an offer in mid-December and was encouraged by the author to start work before the end of December rather than wait until January 2. Although the temptation was great to take time off during the holiday season, she started the new job on December 30. Leslie was well rewarded one year later when annual bonuses were calculated. She received several thousand dollars more for starting in December because a later start would have excluded January from the bonus calculation.

Another example of a start-as-early-as-possible approach benefited a business development manager nine years later! Mike received an offer from a Fortune 500 company on Tuesday, March 15. He immediately took steps to close the deal and determined that Monday, March 21 was the earliest possible start date. His friends urged him to take two weeks off to enjoy himself and to start on April 1, but he resisted and started on the earlier date. He enjoyed a wonderful career until January of his eighth year when the company announced it was merging with another company and offering a "package" to employees who satisfied a minimum criteria of age and years of service. Mike met the age criteria and he needed to reach nine years of company service before March 31. Fortunately, his start date of March 21 nine years earlier allowed him to satisfy the years of service requirement by ten days. He would not have been eligible for this opportunity if he started on April 1.

Due Diligence

The end game is in sight. You have a written offer and you are happy about the terms, your responsibilities, the company, and the employees. This is the time to determine the answer to, "Do I want to work for this company?" It is now safe to ask the sensitive and difficult questions that might have eliminated you from consideration earlier in the interview process. You can ask virtually any questions without impunity so long as they are aimed at enabling you to make an informed decision about the offer. Much of the information you need should have been obtained preparing for the first interview and being a good listener and observer during each interview.

Unleash those bottled up questions that you begrudgingly held back. If you haven't done so, use the web to find investment advice on your potential employer. Check out the company's investor relations data and review SEC reports for public companies and web sites that evaluate public and private companies. The following are some other areas you should be interested in:

➤ Official office hours and those worked by most of the staff

➤ Work space/office/cubicle

➤ PC availability

➤ Company benefits (health, dental, life insurance, 401-K and company contribution, pension plan and vesting, stock options, vacation, etc.) and when they become effective

➤ Title

➤ When bonus is paid and salary reviewed

➤ Administrative support

➤ Background of management team, subordinates, and other key employees

➤ Future prospects of company and its strategic plans for growth

➤ Company research and development efforts

➤ Extent and timing of company-paid training

➤ Expectations your boss has of you in the next 3 to 6 months

➤ Company financial statements, projected profitability, revenue stream

➤ Severance package: duration and components (e.g., salary, benefits)

➤ Relocation package: what will be reimbursed, dollar limit on moving expenses, expiration of relocation offer

During the interview process, one of the most critical things to avoid is volunteering to meet with company staff members not on the original interview list. Additional interviewers can only hurt, not help your candidacy. There is minimal risk now that you have your offer letter. If you have staff reporting to you, or any peer with whom you would work closely, consider requesting a meeting with selected individuals. To initiate such a meeting at this stage of the process is a rare but wise request only if you have serious concerns about joining the company. Expect your new boss to be surprised, but obligated to grant the meeting.

For example, if you have a few or a few hundred people reporting to you, ask your new boss if you could meet your direct reports as a team. Play down the reason for the meeting and state that it is to assess "chemistry" and to begin bonding with your staff and to allow them to feel like being a part of the interview process. Your real reason is to begin your assessment to retain or remove them. If a brief meeting convinces you that a particular person is not competent or easy to work with, you should include in your acceptance discussion that you want the authority to terminate any member of your staff. Another due diligence request you should consider is permission to speak with an outside consultant, venture capitalist, or accountant who has performed work at the company.

Job seekers should also explore unique aspects related to functional areas of expertise. For example, someone who is about to accept a sales position should be sure the company production facility can deliver on your successful sales effort. Many sales staff become former employees voluntarily, or otherwise, when products are only smoke and mirrors. You should also determine the commission structure making certain it is acceptable to you and generous enough to be an incentive to hire additional sales staff.

There are cautions to consider. Do not overdo due diligence. It should be completed quickly, within hours or days, not weeks. A protracted period of time might be viewed by company management as a stalling tactic while you wait for another offer. More than one "chemistry" meeting will be suspect. A successful approach is to ask the hiring manager for permission to discuss company benefits and policies with the HR staff. That discussion should resolve many of your issues. Because there is always a risk that the offer will be withdrawn, perform the minimum amount of due diligence that will provide you with a good feeling for a bright future with the company.

Background Check

When requiring a background check, human resources professionals and hiring managers are taking a prudent step to ensure that new employees are honest and have a good credit rating. A background check can be accomplished for a reasonable fee by one of the many service organizations offering that specialty. These firms require a signed permission or authorization form from the job seeker before a review can be conducted.

Employers can request a service provider to perform selected checks on a job seeker based on responsibilities of the position they are being hired to fill. For example, companies hiring a chief financial officer, or someone who would handle company funds, should ensure at a minimum that the person has a good credit payment history, has no criminal record, and has not recently filed for bankruptcy. If any of these troubles appear on the background report, the job seeker will lose credibility and likely an offer. The same outcome will result for job seekers who lie on applications and résumés. Company management are worried that the same unacceptable behavior traits will carry over to the job. The following are some of the many background checks that can be performed at the discretion of the employer:

Credit History	Criminal and Civil Court Records
Bankruptcy Records	Driving Record
Academic Verification	Professional License Verification
Drug Testing	Reference Checking

Job seekers can take steps to prevent a poor background check from ending up in the hands of a potential employer. The obvious first step is not to lie on résumés or during an interview. If your job requires that you drive a company vehicle and you lied about your poor driving record, you can be sure that when the results of the background check reveal otherwise, you will not get the job. If you are honest and disclose the problem record before the background check is performed, then your potential employer may give you another chance.

The second step you can take is to conduct a background check on yourself at the start of your job search. The cost is reasonable and you will see the reports a potential employer will see. If there are any questionable findings, you have time to correct erroneous information at the credit bureaus or other agencies where you found the less-than-perfect results.

Personality Tests

Personality and psychological assessments have two very different meanings to job seekers. These assessments can be helpful to job seekers looking for suitable career paths based on their favored personality traits. For example, results can help to identify possible professions, job requirements, and level of supervision that are compatible or a good match for a given personality. The term assessment is used for this purpose because publishers advocate that there are no right or wrong answers and the best assessment is made when individuals provide impulsive responses.

Unfortunately for job seekers, these same tools also have a dark side. An increasing number of companies are requiring top candidates to complete a personality assessment as a final interview hurdle before an offer letter becomes binding. Assessments used as an interview criterion are referred to as tests because now there are right and wrong answers that influence a hiring decision. Results are used by HR managers to determine if a candidate matches the desired profile.

For embattled job seekers convinced that the personality test is just another nuisance between them and the job for which they believe to be qualified, this section describes how to nudge test results in their favor. Convince employers that you have the qualities and traits desired, get an offer, and leap over this hurdle to win the interview game. You will have the enviable choice of accepting, negotiating, or rejecting the offer.

What Is Evaluated

Personality tests are used to measure candidate profile and desired personal attributes that appear in the position requirements, while face-to-face interviews ferret out candidate ability to perform required job responsibilities. The following are some of the many personal and personality traits that these tests are designed to measure.

Conscientiousness	Extraversion
Entrepreneurialism	Leadership
Anger	Controlling
Team Player	Openness
Ambition	Flexibility
Detail Oriented	Honesty
Self-Confidence	Customer Orientation
Enthusiasm	Strategic Thinking
Ethical	

The approach for achieving successful test results is the same as for winning the interview—determine the trait or position requirement being evaluated for each question and select the answer that plays to what the company desires in an excellent candidate. Ask the person who informs you of the test for its name or what it is intended to determine. If the person is not forthcoming, use networking contacts or take a best guess to find out what kind of test is to be administered.

Results Can Be What You Want

To a degree . . . according to Dr. Edward Hoffman, a licensed clinical psychologist with 20 years of psychological testing and evaluation experience, in *Ace the Corporate Personality Test.* "But the cold truth is that practice does help. Psychological research has shown that people can effectively alter their performance on personality tests, and that it's not even very difficult."[*] His book, *Ace the Corporate Personality Test,* is an excellent source for job seekers seeking to break through this silent and dreaded gatekeeper.

Regarding possible responses to each question, Dr. Hoffman states "Almost all personality tests use a five-point scale, or occasionally, a seven-point scale. . . possible responses: strongly disagree, disagree, neutral, agree, and strongly agree; . . . .Generally, it's best to avoid checking off the neutral category, which indicates that you lack strong feelings either way about the question."[†]

Each measured trait has a series of statements randomly placed throughout the test, and the answers are summarized as a group to produce a trait assessment on a continuum scale. For example, a common trait that is often assessed is extraversion, and an assessment might fall somewhere on the scale of "strongly extroverted" to "strongly not extroverted," depending on the summary of responses to questions about extraversion.

Practice, Practice, Practice

Math and verbal SAT scores are important differentiators for admission to colleges and universities. Fortunately for high school students, there is an industry of support available to prepare for these tests. Sample questions, coaching services, study guides, and courses provide students with the range of question types and result in reduced anxiety and increased confidence to do well. This level of support is not available when preparing for a personality test that doubles for an interview test. The only exception is when you are told the name of the test in advance. In this fortunate situation, obtain a copy of the test in a bookstore or visit the publisher's web site and practice.

Practice is an effective approach for job seekers to achieve a desired result. The thought process for each question should be to consider the trait being measured and then to select the appropriate re-

---

[*] Edward Hoffman, *Ace the Corporate Personality Test* (New York, McGraw-Hill, 2001), p. 5. Material reproduced with permission of The McGraw-Hill Companies.
[†] Ibid., 28.

sponse that reflects whether you possess the trait or not. Most importantly, disregard instructions to select the first answer that comes to mind. Although this is easier said than done, there are techniques to avoid leaving results to chance.

Always be certain that you understand the meaning of the statement because some use double negatives and must be read more than once, for example, "It is not unlikely that I would have trouble meeting people." Use Internet search engines to find practice tests. Some tests found on the Internet are fee based and others offer free samples and information.

Key words or phrases that produce plenty of search engine results for practicing and learning are "personality tests," "personality assessments," "psychological tests," "psychological assessments," "pre-employment tests," and other words that relate to career or job performance testing. Practice may not make perfect for personality tests, but it should help to move your score into an acceptable range of possessing desired traits.

Lie Scale

Almost all personality tests include embedded questions, known as the lie scale. The responses to these questions are summarized as a group to determine if test takers are intentionally trying to appear more attractive to a prospective employer. If the score for the lie scale indicates the test taker is lying, test results could become suspect and a job offer rescinded. Fortunately, an awareness of these trick questions can help job seekers pass the lie scale and avoid detection of distorting results.

Words that appear in lie scale questions often include all or nothing terms like "always," "never," "all," "everything," and "none." Whenever such absolutes appear in a statement, Dr. Hoffman advises " . . . stay away from either the agree or strongly agree responses for this type of question. On a five-point measure, you'd be wise to indicate a 2—that you moderately disagree with this statement."* The following are sample lie scale statements that should use a level of the disagree response:

---

* Ibid., 31.

➤ I never fail to meet deadlines.

➤ I always enjoy the challenges of new projects.

➤ People I meet are interested in everything I say.

➤ None of my peers enjoy working with me.

➤ I liked every course I took.

Another type of question similar to a lie scale group assesses the consistency of your responses on a particular topic. For example, if you responded in one question that you preferred the outdoors and related activities, all other responses regarding outdoor activities should be "agree" or "strongly agree" with an interest in the outdoor activity.

Measured Traits

Dr. Hoffman identifies seven traits that employers want to assess—conscientiousness, extraversion, anger, integrity, entrepreneurialism, stress, and leadership. "The most important predictor of job performance has been identified as conscientiousness."* Job seekers are safe to assume that no employer wants new-hires to be anything less than conscientious.

As you read each question or statement, ask yourself if the question is trying to measure how you rate as a conscientious person and select the appropriate response to convey that you are very conscientious. Similar qualities associated with "conscientious" include methodical, careful, reliable, thorough, orderly, meticulous, precise, punctual, well prepared, and exact. Completing assigned tasks and fulfilling responsibilities are the basis of other questions that evaluate conscientious. The best approach to achieve the desired score for each trait being measured is to take sample personality tests that explain the appropriate response for each statement.

Ace the Corporate Personality Test provides the reader with six sample personality tests, identifies the respective statements

---

* Ibid., 37.

that measure the seven popular traits identified in the book, and enables the reader to determine the best response for each question. The book also lists a series of statements, appropriate responses, and rationale for each of the seven traits. For example, the following five statements with respective rationales measure conscientiousness[*]:

1. "The most successful people are those who always complete what they begin."

   You want to *strongly agree* with this sort of statement in order to show your conscientiousness. Your role models should be those who finish whatever they start.

2. "I know many people who work themselves too hard."

   On personality tests for hiring, there's nothing more valued than hard work, and workaholics don't exist. A *strongly disagree* response is therefore advised.

3. "Employees should not generally be expected to work extra hours to finish a job on time."

   A sign of your conscientiousness is precisely your willingness to work additional hours. So *strongly disagree* is an advisable response.

4. "If I have to work late, or on a weekend, I usually feel bothered a little."

   Remember, you want to present yourself as someone who does whatever is necessary to complete a task. So it's advisable to *disagree* or *strongly disagree* with this item.

5. "Most people consider me very reliable if something needs to be done promptly."

   Reliability is a prime element in conscientiousness. You certainly want to *strongly agree* with this statement.

Extraversion is another widely evaluated trait versus its counterpart introversion. The following are five questions with response that Dr. Hoffman uses to illustrate an extraverted person[†]:

---

[*] Ibid., 39, 41, 43.
[†] Ibid., 47–51.

1. "I almost never feel bored at parties."
    Remember, extraverts love parties, so they would *strongly agree* with all such statements.

2. "In conversations, I like to let the other person do most of the talking."
    Extraverts typically dominate conversations, so the appropriate response is *strongly disagree*.

3. "Almost none of my friends are quiet and reserved."
    Usually, our friends resemble us personality-wise, so the fitting response is *strongly agree* for an extravert.

4. "I am a very easy person to get to know."
    Extraverts are typically open with their feelings and moods, so the correct response is *strongly agree*.

5. "I sometimes avoid meeting new groups of people."
    Extraverts would say the opposite, and thus *strongly disagree* with this statement.

Become familiar with these tests to minimize the shock of your personality being explored for the first time. Learn test formats and rules. Familiarity should reduce anxiety and the possible anger that these tests sometimes arouse when it becomes an interview requirement. Use your networking skills to find and talk with others who have completed these tests and review the test developer's web site. Determine what traits the test is designed to measure. Be aware of the lie scale and provide consistent answers regarding traits being measured. Take a moment to think about each question and provide the answer that satisfies the desired trait required for the position. Disregard the hiring company request to provide the first answer that comes to your mind. Finally, practice with sample tests.

Susan Is Still in the Game

Almost a month had passed since Susan's second interview when she saw Scott's Caller ID on her cell phone. Because there was no recruiter involved, she will rely on Scott to be the intermediary between her and the VP-marketing. Following a few minutes of small talk, Scott gets right to the point. You impressed everyone and we would like to go the next step and check three references. We narrowed the search down from almost 250 candidates to just two—you and one other. If we can speak with all the references this week, then we will make our decision next week. Susan expressed her excitement and continued interest in the position. It was mid-afternoon and she told Scott that by the morning he would receive contact information for three references.

References

This was good news. Susan had one competitor to eliminate and her only weapon at this time was to select stellar references and be certain that they were well prepared. She worked three years at her recent company and decided to select two members of senior management—her boss (the VP-marketing) and the president. Her third reference was the president of another publishing firm with which she negotiated a marketing alliance. Alliances will be an integral part of her new responsibilities and a previous partner would be perfect to demonstrate her competency in that area. Two presidents and a vice president are excellent choices for references.

Susan immediately called each reference to alert them about a call and to let them know the urgent need for their response. She identified key areas for each to emphasize. The president of her recent firm was asked to expand on her professionalism and the trust the president placed in her to explore alliances with other publishers and to serve as a speaker at industry conferences. The VP-marketing was asked to describe Susan's in-depth knowledge of membership-based businesses and her experience working with ad agencies, which was a requirement Susan surfaced in her first interview with Scott. The third reference was asked to describe Susan's negotiating ability and professionalism.

After a brief discussion with each, she sent an e-mail outlining the information required for the upcoming call. Susan then sent Scott the contact information. Within two days, the three references called her to summarize the results of their discussion with Scott. Everything appeared to be going well. Again, Susan must wait.

The Offer

The call came the next week as Scott indicated. It was three months after Susan's friend Tom referred her.

Scott: Susan, your references were impeccable and we would like you to join our marketing team. Our compensation package consists of a base salary plus annual bonus and company benefits. We would like to offer you $78,000 plus a 25% bonus based on the performance of both you and the company. Your title will be director of marketing reporting to the VP-marketing. The reason we conducted such an extensive search is because the position we are offering you is targeted at moving into the VP-marketing position when Tara takes over one of our subsidiaries in the next year or so. Well, what's your reaction?

Susan: That is just wonderful, Scott. I am really ecstatic. Would you please fax or e-mail an offer letter and I will be back to you in a day? Also, who can I call for information on company benefits?

Scott: Terrific. I will fax an offer letter within an hour and I will tell Marsha, our Compensation and Benefits Manager, to expect your call. By the way, I will also send you a permission form for us to do a background check which we do for all new employees. I hope you will accept the offer and join us. Please let me know a start date when you call tomorrow. Thanks.

Within an hour Susan received her offer letter, which included a respectable 10% increase over her previous salary. The background check was a surprise, but she had nothing to worry about because she was totally honest about her degree and all the information she provided Scott. She was very relieved that there was no personality test.

Susan called Scott the next morning. She had one question related to the company's profitability and revenue stream since it is a private company. Scott replied with a reassuring answer. Susan then weighed the risk of negotiating for a higher base and the possibility of losing the offer even at this late stage. What convinced her to make the first move to negotiate was the excellent rapport she developed with Scott. She knew her request must be done in a professional, non-demanding manner. "Scott, you know how excited I am about this offer, and I would like to ask if there is room in the budget for a base of $81,000?" Scott was apologetic in his reply and said "We can't go a penny over $80,000. Would that be acceptable?" Another winning move by Susan. She accepted the offer immediately. Susan took the initiative to inform Scott that she would like to start on Monday, just five days away. Scott agreed and Susan will be the official winner of the interview game when she appears at her new job on Monday morning.

An acceptance letter sent to your new supervisor in advance of your start date conveys a professional image and contributes to a warm impression. Susan sends an e-mail to her new boss, the VP-marketing, stating how pleased she is to receive the offer and that she looks forward to being a productive member of the team.

Transition from Interviewee to Employee

The first day at your new job is a surreal experience filled with exhilaration, apprehension, and many challenges that you convinced interviewers you can solve. You have just become a player in a new game—The Corporate Survival Game. Before you sit at your new desk on that soon-to-be memorable first day, you should have a plan to survive in your new company as long as circumstances permit. Starting a new job provides you with more control over your future than you had as a job seeker. Take advantage of your current situation and be proactive to ensure success in your new job and in the next interview game.

You are about to enter the world of company politics and the need to impress everyone you meet. The same qualities applied in the interview game plus unbounded energy must now be directed towards living up to and exceeding the expectations of those who hired you.

Preparation for the First Day

If this activity sounds like you read about it a few chapters ago, you are right. In the first weeks of your new job, you will be interviewing with every employee in your department or office location. If the company is small, you might meet every employee, and you must be ready for each one. The preparation and due diligence you performed when interviewing should be immensely helpful for this new and important purpose. In most instances, many employees will have the perception that you are able to "hit the ground running" on the first day. Do not disappoint them.

On her first day, Verity, the new information technology project manager, entered the reception area of her new company and introduced herself as the newly hired project manager. The HR director was supposed to welcome her, but he was called away to an emergency meeting. Fortunately, the HR director informed the receptionist to call the vice president-information technology, Barry, with whom Verity previously interviewed. Barry immediately went to the reception area and apologized for the absence of the HR director. There was no office space available and Barry walked Verity to a temporary location—a conference table in the CEO's office. The CEO was out of town for the week.

Verity took all this in stride. When Barry asked Verity if she needed anything, she realized that there was no formal orientation program and she would have to orchestrate her own introduction to company employees. One key need Verity identified during her interviews was that the company expected her to improve a financial system with the chief financial officer (CFO) being the key user. She asked Barry if she could be introduced to the CFO and Barry gladly made the introduction in the first hour of the first day. Verity focused on her first impression skills and established rapport with the CFO. She then asked the CFO if he could describe the financial system and provide her with the requirements for improving it. The CFO was very impressed. Verity's initiative left those who met her with the impression that she fits right in with other employees and was off to a running start.

During the honeymoon phase of a new job, a conscious effort should be made to ensure long-term success. The interview technique of uncovering the interviewer's needs must be executed with virtually every person you meet for the first time. After making the first impression and establishing rapport, ask how you can help each person from your position on the organization chart or from a personal standpoint. This offer should be a major contributor to the first impression. Take note of the response and be sincere in your effort to assist other employees in the weeks and months ahead.

Stand Out from the Crowd

One of the most significant steps to ensure a lasting success in a new company is to identify and accomplish something significant that would benefit the company within the first 3 to 6 weeks. It is important to identify a critical company or department need during the orientation period when you meet other employees.

Another reason for an early accomplishment is the recruiter's guarantee period under which you are required to remain with the company. If you should leave voluntarily or be terminated during this period, the recruiter must return the fee or replace you at no cost. Be assured that the VP-HR is watching the calendar for that date to arrive, and the weeks prior are very dangerous for newly hired job seekers. Ask the recruiter when the guarantee period ends and plan to deliver results prior to that date. The guarantee period for contingency recruiters is generally 30, 60, or 90 days, while it may be one or two years for a retained firm. You should also ask the recruiter to suggest what would be an impressive accomplishment.

Some examples of a major accomplishment might be (1) to introduce one of your supervisors to a member of the management team at a potential customer, (2) to provide someone on the senior management team with an opportunity to be a guest speaker at a prestigious industry conference, (3) to identify and deliver a real, unexpected revenue opportunity, or (4) to identify a significant cost savings that can be realized immediately without creating enemies in the process. Identifying such an accomplishment is often as difficult as achieving it.

Ron was hired as a technology systems support manager in the help desk department. During the interview process, he was told by another technical staff member that the department needed a control program to track user troubleshooting requests. The week before he started his new job, Ron wrote a program that he thought would keep track of the department's troubleshooting projects. He waited two weeks to get acclimated to the new environment and updated the program to include requirements he uncovered on the job. He casually discussed the project with his supervisor who thought it was an excellent idea. Within the next week, Ron finalized the program and presented it to his supervisor. The supervisor was very impressed with Ron and his self-directed project. By the end of the third week of employment, Ron was in the office of the vice president of his department receiving praise for his initiative and quality work. A great start to a new job.

Senior Management

As a general rule, anyone higher than you on the organization chart can help to catapult you up or out of the organization. The first person to impress and demonstrate that the company made the right choice to hire you is your immediate supervisor. Meet with this person in your first week after all benefit forms, security badges, pass to the company store, and other administrative matters are completed. The purpose of this meeting is to determine what is expected of you in the first three to six months of employment. Document all deliverables with expected due dates, a description of what the results should look like, where and from whom you would obtain the data, and the purpose of each deliverable. Be careful not to assume too much responsibility too soon as part of the euphoria of a new job.

Interview your immediate supervisor to assess personality, determine if there is an open door to ask questions, and evaluate how close their relationship is to senior management. Establish or solidify a rapport as you did in Chapter 2.

Confirm that your supervisor is the person who submits a request for your pay raise and bonus and ask for a clarification of how performance will be measured, when raises are determined, and who the key influencers are. Learn how and how frequently your supervisor likes to be updated on progress and the extent to which you can make decisions without approval. As a summary of this first and important meeting, you should document your agreed-upon deliverables and due dates and send a copy to your supervisor as acknowledgement that you are actively working on the near-term projects. A final outcome of this meeting should be an announcement from your supervisor or the human resources head welcoming you to the staff and describing your responsibilities. Leave no room for gossip about what you were hired to do.

Determine who the major influencers are, i.e., those who will evaluate your work and inform your supervisor how you performed. Meet with these individuals periodically; establish rapport and a supportive working relationship. Key questions to ask each influencer are primary business needs and how you can help to make them successful in their corporate role. If you are lucky, a mutual respect will develop with one of these influencers and the person will become a mentor.

Peer Group

Most employees joining a new company become a member of a peer group including those who work for the same supervisor and/or are at the same level in another department. Although most members of a peer group will welcome you to help share the workload, there might be one or two members who feel threatened and are concerned you will take over their job. Reach out to these individuals who might have a tendency to undermine your accomplishments by demonstrating a sharing and giving attitude. Offer information without being asked and assist wherever possible. Be viewed as a supportive team player.

Take the initiative to meet with each peer and determine responsibilities, background, reporting relationships, and what each is recognized and respected for doing. Identify their important business needs and vocal complaints. Be a good listener. Keep your focus on the personal deliverables in your work plan and on that special accomplishment you are looking to achieve.

Subordinates

The first thought of any subordinate upon learning that a new boss has been hired is that their job is in jeopardy or there will be a major organizational change, neither of which is something to look forward to. Do not give any assurances to your staff in the first weeks on the job. The best you can do is to reassure each person that you will focus on individual strengths and try to satisfy personal needs and interests.

Do not expect unquestioned loyalty from your new staff until you establish credibility and gain their respect. Until that occurs, you may have disgruntled employees in your group. If one of them falls in the category of influencer, then you can expect some trouble. Pam faced this problem when she assumed responsibility for the accounting staff in her first week on the job. It took Pam about two months to realize that her supervisor was aware of some difficult staffing issues that he did not discuss with her. During her third month on the job, she had lunch with a group of her peers and a startling revelation was made. Pam's accounts payable clerk was the CEO's cousin. Pam had a gossiping influencer lurking in her group. She began to filter her conversations at team meetings.

Culture

When organizations can be characterized in certain ways, then you can describe the culture in the same terms. For example, some companies are considered to be very conservative where men wear a dark suit, white shirt, and tie, and women dress in comparable attire. Employees at dotcom companies proudly wore jeans to the office. Some companies had a reputation for its consultants being arrogant and overly confident, while other organizations are known for their analysis-paralysis when making decisions.

Culture is something not learned in a day or at an orientation program. It is a cumulative knowledge gained through time served. Determine the culture however it can be defined. Are all employees very polite and respectful? Are there many memos written to document every moment of the working day? What are the generally accepted arrival and departure times adhered to by most employees? Is there terminology unique to the company? Does the company have a motto? Are there mentors to whom new employees can turn for advice?

Avoid personal and sensitive discussions with other staff. Topics to avoid are religion and politics—expression of personal views can easily be a path to creating enemies in the crucial first weeks of employment. If forced into a discussion, be vague, be polite, and create an excuse to leave the conversation. Do not attempt to change company culture. Arrive at 8 A.M. if everyone else does and blend into the existing environment as if you have been there for years.

Find a Mentor

As a personal 'board of directors' should have provided needed support during your search, you should identify a company mentor in the first months of a new job to provide a different kind of support. The right mentor can help you to be successful technically, emotionally, or politically in your new job. Workers early in their career may require someone with extensive experience in the same field to whom they can turn for assistance with difficult problems. Other areas in which a mentor can help are: 1) to speak up on your behalf at company meetings which you do not attend, 2) to educate you about company politics, 3) to introduce you to company power players, and 4) to provide advice.

Mentors should hold a more senior position than you and should not work for your immediate supervisor. A good choice for a mentor would be at least one level above your immediate supervisor, preferably in another department. Ideally, the mentor should be an officer of the company and a person with some influence over decision-making at the senior management level. If you are a vice president and report to the CEO, seek someone on the board, if you are below the vice president level, then a vice president would be an excellent choice.

When you identify someone you would like as a mentor, seek opportunities to attend the same meetings, sit at the same table in the company cafeteria, or be creative to arrange an introduction. A first meeting with your chosen mentor should be treated as a first meeting with an interviewer. Make that first impression and establish rapport. Once rapport is established, and you will know when that happens, you have succeeded in finding your mentor.

Prepare for the Next Interview Game

You should be ready to become a player in the interview game at any moment just like a great martial artist is in a state of constant preparedness. During periods of travel in dark and suspicious alleyways the awareness level is on high alert. As it should be with you when company profits plunge or there is a change of management. Worse yet, if you are terminated, you should be in a position to spring into the interview game and strive for a quick win. What should you be doing to prepare for the next interview game?

Thank Your Network

In the week before your first day on the new job, review the list of networking contacts you developed during your search and complete any to-dos. You should prepare your database of contacts for a mass mail-merge with personally addressed letters. These letters, or emails, should thank your contacts for the assistance offered during your search and state that you would welcome an opportunity to re-ciprocate in any way possible and at any time. The letters should state your new company, position, and contact information.

In addition to friends and business associates, recruiters should be informed of your new job. Offer to be a source for recruiter searches and indicate that you have greatly expanded your network in the past few months and will likely have a referral or two. This offer will keep lines of communication open with the recruiter channel for future job opportunities because recruiters pride themselves on the number of sitting executives and employed individuals who fill their database.

The close circle of contacts directly responsible for introducing you to the new company, serving as references, and assisting you in other ways deserve a special thank-you. This should take the form of a warm, handwritten thank-you note, and a special gift or a celebration lunch or dinner, depending on the amount of help offered.

These letters should be sent after you have been on the job at least two weeks. It is prudent to ensure that you are fully on the payroll and at your own desk before you inform a large circle of contacts.

Keep Your Résumé Ready

If you have any desire to inquire about another job opportunity or if you must quickly mobilize a new job search, you will require an up-dated résumé. The source of input for any résumé updates should be your new job accomplishments. Keep track of each accomplishment in résumé format with the problem you addressed, the action you took, and the result achieved. After six months in a new job your accomplishments should be impressive. Update your work-in-process résumé every four to six months.

Continue to Network

Complacency is the enemy of newly hired employees so be aware of its symptoms. Most winners of the interview game realize that the majority of new jobs are the direct result of a personal network, not recruiters, ads, or direct mail campaigns. Your goal upon starting a new job is not only to maintain the recent network you built, but to increase it substantially and to have a far larger network ready when needed.

Throughout your career you should reach out to meet new people, build relationships, and keep the existing network alive. Contact manager software should become your most valuable asset as you continue to populate its database with new names. Attend cocktail parties, be a guest speaker at conferences, and make luncheon appointments. Meet with industry experts and peers at other companies to learn new ideas for your current company and to establish working relationships. The rewards of developing a large network will be realized both professionally and personally.

Establish Recruiter Relationships

Shortly after you start a new job, an interesting phenomenon occurs. Recruiters will appear out of nowhere and you will be getting the calls you worked so hard to get while a job seeker. Recruiters typically call employed individuals as potential candidates for a search, as a source for potential candidates, or as a potential recruiting client. Regardless of the reason, you are in a different place than you were as a job seeker. A recruiter-initiated call provides you with the rare opportunity to establish a relationship. Listen to the search opportunity and present yourself if interested or provide names of possible candidates if not interested. Recruiters remember those who assist with a search. Establish rapport, obtain all contact information, and enter it into your contact database.

Be Supportive

The basic tenet of networking is the more you help others, the more you will be helped. Consider the time you were looking for a job and repeatedly left messages for someone recommended by a friend. That was not a cold call and you should have gotten a courteous response. Do not ignore a caller if recommended by an acquaintance. Make this person part of your network and you will become part of theirs. The term "what goes around comes around" must have been coined for networking purposes. You will certainly remember the names of referred contacts who never returned your call, especially when one of them calls you a year later looking for assistance. Be proactive, supportive, and responsive when approached by job seekers —everyone can become a winner.

Good luck.

APPENDIX

JOB SEEKER CHECKLIST FOR WINNING THE INTERVIEW GAME

1. Prepare for an upcoming interview.

2. Understand recruiter and human resources perspectives—the gatekeepers.

3. Develop a relaxing and confident mind-set on the morning of interview.

4. Be alert while waiting in the reception area.

5. Make a great first impression with each interviewer.

6. Establish rapport in the first fifteen minutes and build it throughout the interview.

7. Respond to interview questions in a winning way and ask some of your own.

8. Attempt tactics to change negative interviewer behavior when necessary.

9. Neutralize age, frequent job changes, and other difficult issues.

10. Complement a first impression with a lasting impression at the end of each interview.

11. Summarize notes immediately after each interview.

12. Send thank you notes within one day.

13. Determine how you can differentiate yourself from other candidates.

14. Obtain and use competitive candidate intelligence effectively.

15. Respond carefully to preliminary job offer inquiries.

16. Select the right references and prepare each reference when you are requested to submit names.

17. Move personality test results in your favor.

18. Negotiate your offer and use multiple offers as leverage.

19. Transition from interviewee to employee.

20. Prepare for the next interview game.

BIBLIOGRAPHY

(The accuracy of the contents of the cited resources cannot be guaranteed. Web sites are provided for reader convenience and do not constitute an endorsement.)

Company, Industry and Career Resources

www.aarp.org.   Career and other resources for anyone 50 or over.

www.acinet.org   America's Career Infonet provides online career resources, wages and employment trends, and more.

www.ajb.dni.us/   America's Job Bank includes online job database and career resources.

www.business.com   Business-focused search engine designed to find information on industries, companies, products, and services.

www.careerbuilder.com   Includes a job database and career advice.

www.careerxroads.com   Publishes a reference guide to online job resources and more.

www.ceoexpress.com/default.asp   Provides users with an extensive collection of business research, daily news and much more.

www.Eliyon.com   A subscription-based service that provides access to a database of people and companies.

www.execunet.com   Internet-based career management resource for senior executives earning $100K+, including online job database, career advice and more.

http://fcke.fastcompany.com/   Fast Company has a company research directory and much more.

www.Forbes.com   Publication includes business and financial information, lists of top companies, and more.

www.fortune.com/fortune/   Provides business, company, and financial news.

www.fuld.com   Fuld & Company provides business and competitive intelligence for a wide range of industries.

www.hoovers.com/free/   Provides company and other business information.

http://hotjobs.yahoo.com/   Online job database and career tools.

www.inc.com/inc500   Provides Inc 500 company lists.

www.industryweek.com/   Provides company profiles and other business information.

www.job.com   Online jobs database and career resource.

www.monster.com/   Online jobs database, company and career resource.

www.netshare.com/   Provides online job listings, networking opportunities and career management resources for the $100K+ executive.

www.salary.com   Provides job descriptions and salary for occupations in its files.

www.sec.gov/   Securities and Exchange Commission includes public company filings.

State web sites for researching companies, jobs and other information. Enter www.state.STATE.us/, where STATE is the 2-character state abbreviation (e.g., www.state.CA.us for California).

www.bls.gov/oco/   U.S. Department of Labor, Bureau of Labor Statistics. Occupational Outlook Handbook for numerous occupations providing working conditions, required training and education, earnings and expected job prospects.

www.weddles.com/   Publishes *Weddle's Guide to Employment Web Sites*, and other job seeker resources.

www.zapdata.com   Includes business information, mailing lists, company, industry, and information.

Neuro Linguistic Programming and Rapport

Bandler, Richard, and John Grinder. *Frogs into Princes: Neuro Linguistic Programming*. Moab, Utah: Real People Press, 1979.

Brooks, Michael. *Instant Rapport*. New York: Warner Books, 1989.

Charvet, Shelle Rose. *Words That Change Minds, Mastering the Language of Influence*. Dubuque: Kendall/Hunt Publishing Company, 1997.

Knight, Sue. *NLP Solutions: How to Model What Works in Business to Make it Work for You*. Naperville: Nicholas Brealey Publishing Limited, 1999.

Laborde, Genie. *Influencing with Integrity: Management Skills for Communication and Negotiation*. Palo Alto: Syntony Publishing, 2001. See http://www.influence-integrity.com/index.htm.

Laborde, Genie. *Fine Tune Your Brain, When Everything's Going Right and What To Do When It Isn't*. Palo Alto: Syntony Publishing, 1988.

Lewis, Byron, and Frank Pucelik. *Magic of NLP Demystified*. Portland: Metamorphous Press, 1990.

Merrill, M. "Sharpening Your Interviewing Skills." Merrill Associates, Columbus, Ohio, 2000. http://www.merrillassociates.net/topicofthe month.php?topic=200010_2.

Nierenberg, Gerard, and Henry Calero. *How to Read a Person Like a Book, The Classic Guide to Interpreting Body Language*. New York: Simon & Schuster, Inc., 1986.

O'Connor, J. and J. Seymour (contributor). *Introducing Neuro-Linguistic Programming: The New Psychology of Personal Excellence*. London: HarperCollins Publishers, 1990.

Personality and Assessment

Buckingham, Marcus, and Donald O. Clifton. *Now, Discover Your Strengths*. New York: The Free Press, 2001.

Hoffman, Edward. *Ace the Corporate Personality Test*. New York: Mc-Graw Hill, 2001.

Jansen, Julie. *I Don't Know What I Want, but I Know It's Not This: A Step-by-Step Guide to Finding Gratifying Work*. New York: Penguin Books, 2003.

Keirsey, David. *Please Understand Me II*. Del Mar, Calif.: Prometheus Nemesis Book Company, 1998.

Lore, Nicholas. *The Pathfinder, How to Choose or Change Your Career for a Lifetime of Satisfaction and Success*. New York: Simon & Schuster, 1998.

Myers, Isabel Briggs with Peter Briggs Myers. *Gifts Differing: Understanding Personality Type*. Mountain View, CA. Davies-Black Publishing, Division of Consulting Psychologists Press (CPP), Inc., 1995. http://www.mbti.com/.

Tieger, Paul D., and Barbara Barron-Tieger. *Do What You Are: Discover the Perfect Career for You Through the Secrets of Personality Type*. Boston: Little, Brown and Company, 2001. www.personalitytype.com.

U.S. Department of Labor's O*NET Project. *Testing and Other Assessments: Helping You Make Better Career Decisions*. Washington, D.C., 1999. http://www.careertools.org/pdf/00-testother.pdf.

U.S. Department of Labor. *Employment and Training Administration, Skills Assessment and Analysis Program*. O*NET Project, *Testing and Assessment: An Employer's Guide to Good Practices*. Washington, D.C., 2000. http://www.onetcenter.org/dl_files/empTestAsse.pdf.

http://www.personalitypathways.com/.   Contains descriptive information about personality types and other helpful information.

INDEX